Preserving History

The Construction of History in the K-16 Classroom

Preserving History

The Construction of History in the K-16 Classroom

Scott Monroe Waring
University of Central Florida

Information Age Publishing, Inc.
Charlotte, North Carolina • www.infoagepub.com

Library of Congress Cataloging-in-Publication Data

Waring, Scott Monroe.
  Preserving history : the construction of history in the K-16 classroom /
Scott Monroe Waring.
       p. cm.
  Includes bibliographical references.
  ISBN 978-1-61735-381-9 (paperback) — ISBN 978-1-61735-382-6 (hardcover) — ISBN 978-1-61735-383-3 (e-book)
  1. History—Study and teaching (Primary) 2. History—Study and teaching (Secondary) 3. History—Study and teaching (Higher) I. Title.
  D16.2.W34 2011
  907.1—dc22

                                                                2011001321

Copyright © 2011 IAP–Information Age Publishing, Inc.

All rights reserved. No part of this publication may be reproduced, stored in a retrieval system, or transmitted in any form or by any electronic or mechanical means, or by photocopying, microfilming, recording or otherwise without written permission from the publisher.

Printed in the United States of America

CONTENTS

1. **Introduction** 1

2. **Teaching History Literature** 7
   Transfer of Knowledge 8
   Historical Thinking and Inquiry in the Classroom 9
   Disciplined/Historical Inquiry 11

3. **Developing Historical Thinking Skills** 15
   What is a Historian and What are Primary Sources? 16
   Analyzing Primary Sources 19
   Multiple Perspectives of Historical Events 22
   Perspectives 24
   Engaging in an Authentic Historical Assessment Activity 26
   Conclusion 28

4. **Multiple Presentations of History:**
   The Battle of Lexington Green 29

5. **Historical Causality** 37

6. **Building Historical Agency** 43
   Four Core Features to Human Agency 46
   Different Modes of Human Agency:
      Personal, Proxy, and Collective 46
   Teaching / Historical Agency 47
   Internet/Agency 48
      Personal Agency and the Internet 49
      Proxy Agency and the Internet 49
      Collective Agency and the Internet 51

v

      Example and Instructional Guide 53
      Conclusion 53

7. Utilizing Methods of Interest to Digital Natives **55**
      Utilizing Sources Other Than Traditional Web Sites:
          Online Auctions 57
      Timelines for Building Historical Understanding 61
      Virtual History: Inserting sTudents Back Into the Past 62
      Conclusion 68

**8. Engaging in Authentic Historical Inquiry
by Investigating History Close to the Learner
(Local History)** **69**
      Oral Histories 71
      Walking Tours or Bus Tours 74
      Buildings 75
      Cemeteries and Headstones 75
      Business Partnerships, Local Historical Associations,
          and Museums 77
      Artifacts 78
      Photographs 78
      Postcards and Greeting Cards 81
      Radio 82
      Community Service Projects 82
      Final Products 83
      Conclusion 86

9. Conclusion **89**

References **91**

About the Author **109**

CHAPTER 1

INTRODUCTION

What and how to teach in the K-16 history classroom has been a perennial and, at times, heated debate. Beginning as early as 1892, the question of what knowledge is of the most worth and what should be the central function of the history curriculum became a focus of many interested in education. In this year, the National Education Association constructed the Committee of Ten to examine college entrance requirements, including levels of historical knowledge. Many, at the time, felt that "no subject so widely taught is, on the whole, taught so poorly" (Hall, 1885, p. ix). The committee's task focused upon how to teach history, while meeting societal demands of a changing nation and curricular needs of and for the citizens within it (Kleibard, 2004). The subgroup of the Committee of Ten that focused on history education, the "Madison Conference," posited that students needed a minimum of 8 years of history coursework, including history courses at each of the four grade levels in high school. They suggested that students have numerous and varied opportunities to cultivate the powers of observation, to follow arguments and make discriminative judgments, and to use various historical sources, as frequently as possible (U.S. Bureau of Education, 1893). It was felt that the teachers needed to move away from "traditional" methods of teaching history, such as rote memorization and the "dry and lifeless system of instruction by text-book," and find new and engaging ways to "broaden and cultivate the mind." Unfortunately, these recommendations faced many critics and did not take hold in K-16 classrooms at this time or, frankly, at any point since then.

In 1917, J. Carleton Bell noted that, from his experience speaking with history teachers at all levels of education, one thought persisted. He heard teachers saying, "I do not care to have my pupils learn dates and events, but I am particularly anxious to have them develop the historic sense." As he questioned what this meant, especially for the learner in a history classroom, he utilized a description by an eminent university professor of history who summed up this thought:

> If two students are given a number of newspaper files and are asked to write the history of a town for a 5-year period, one will give a clear, intelligible, well articulated account, with the various events and movements in due perspective, with adequate emphasis on a few leading features and proper subordination of details, while the other will have merely a hodge-podge of miscellaneous facts. The one shows the historic sense, the other does not. (pp. 317-318)

In a companion study, which was the first large-scale test of factual knowledge in U.S. history, Bell and his colleague David F. McCollum (1917) revealed results indicating that, of the 1,500 Texas students examined, 16% in the upper three grades of the elementary level (middle grades), 33% at the high school level, and 49% at the college level were able to correctly answer "simple" questions about fundamental aspects of U.S. history. They affirmed that this does not show a very thorough mastery of basic historical facts. Although the results were discouraging, they offered, within this study, five aspects of the historic sense that should be a part of an examination of a history classroom and the students' abilities. These included:

1. The ability to understand present events in light of the past.
2. Skill in sifting and evaluating a mass of miscellaneous materials, such as newspaper stories, contemporary documents, hearsay reports, partisan attacks, and special pleadings, and constructing from this confused tangle a straightforward and probable account of a series of events in their causal and consequential relationships.
3. The appreciation and comprehension of a simple historical narrative.
4. Reflective and discriminating replies to "thought questions" on a given historical situation.
5. The readiness with which pupils answer questions revealing the range of their historical information (pp. 257-258).

The first four aspects are vital keys to allowing students an opportunity to engage in historical thought and inquiry and building historic sense. Unfortunately, continued controversy, at this time over what students should be taught, overshadowed these proposed approaches to the teaching of history. Bell and McCollum admitted that the fifth aspect was the narrowest and possibly the least important, but they noted that this was the one that was most frequently assessed. Not much has changed in the years since this was published, nearly a century ago.

The headline in the *New York Times* on April 4, 1943, alerted the American home front that there was an "Ignorance of U.S. History Shown by College Freshmen" (Fine, 1943). An examination of 7,000 college freshmen, across 36 institutions of higher education, provided evidence of this lack of historical knowledge and, more commonly, misinformation. Only 6% of the participants could name the original 13 colonies, with nearly every one of the current 50 states being listed at least once. A greater number of respondents listed Theodore Roosevelt than William McKinley as the president during the Spanish-American War, only 25% knew that Abraham Lincoln was the president during the American Civil War, nearly 50% identified Andrew Jackson as "Stonewall" Jackson, more than 40 names were listed as the president at some point in American history who never served in that capacity, and only 22% of them could list two contributions made by Abraham Lincoln. With nearly 82% of colleges and universities not requiring any American history, the author, Benjamin Fine, suggested that one way to remedy this was to require all students to take a course in this "important field." Allan Nevins, professor of history at Columbia University, critiqued that "we cannot understand what we are fighting for unless we know how our principles developed."

The Educational Testing Service's 42-question, multiple-choice test (1976) showed that, of the 1,856 college freshman surveyed across 194 campuses, students averaged 21 correct, which equates to a score of 50% (Fiske, 1976). Results from the 1987, 1994, 2001, and 2006 U.S. history reports of the National Assessment of Educational Progress (known informally as the "Nation's Report Card") have shown little deviation from earlier trends. Thus, even though we tend to have a nostalgic memory of earlier time periods and, in turn, the educational capabilities of the children from various times in our nation's past, the results from studies examining the historical knowledge base of America's youth has remained fairly constant.

Much of the lack of knowledge stems from the manner in which history is traditionally taught, which is typically an approach that follows a schedule like: Monday, read the chapter; Tuesday, complete vocabulary for the chapter; Wednesday, complete questions at the back of the book; Thursday, prepare for the quiz; and Friday, take the quiz. These sorts of methods greatly impact the interest levels, or more frequently the distaste, generated for learning about historical content and, thus, the public's corresponding perception of the importance of history within the K-16 curriculum. In a national survey conducted by Roy Rosenzweig and David Thelen (1998), with assistance from the Indiana University's Center for Survey Research, 808 Americans were surveyed and were asked to "pick one word or phrase to describe your experience with history classes in elementary or high school." "Boring" was the single most frequent description, and negative descriptions significantly outweighed positive ones. This is the prevailing thought, presented by respondents in various surveys and studies, about history instruction and its importance. It is vital that history instruction moves away from the typical model of history instruction, one described as being an approach of "persistent instruction," which involves a single teacher lecturing for the entire class period in front of a group of 25-40 students (Cuban, 1982).

In addition, teachers cannot approach history instruction with assumptions such as, "If I said it, that means they learned it!", "You can't teach students how to think until you've taught them what to think," and that "I may be doing it wrong, but I am doing it in the proper and customary way" (Calder, 2006). David McCullough (2005) stated it nicely:

> History is a natural human interest, and to make it boring, to make it dull, to make it insipid or sleep inducing is really a shame, a tragedy. The great thing about history is that it is about life. Every time you scratch the surface of the supposedly dead past, you find life, and you learn.

The question then is "How do we accomplish effective history instruction without boring the students?" The Bradley Commission on History in Schools (1995) suggested that history teaching must allow students to:

- understand the significance of the past;
- distinguish between the important and the inconsequential;
- develop historical empathy as opposed to present-mindedness;
- acquire at one and the same time a comprehension of diverse cultures and of shared humanity;
- understand how things happen and how things change;
- comprehend the interplay of change and continuity;
- prepare to live with uncertainties;
- grasp the complexity of historical causation, respect particularity, and avoid excessively abstract generalizations;
- appreciate the often tentative nature of judgments about the past;

- recognize the importance of individuals who have made a difference in history;
- appreciate the force of the nonrational, the irrational, and the accidental;
- understand the relationship between geography and history as a matrix of time and place; and
- read widely and critically.

These guidelines assist teachers in moving away from what Sam Wineburg calls the "attic theory" of cognition (Calder, 2006). As he has noted, learners do not collect facts the way people collect furniture or heirlooms, storing pieces away in the attic or storage unit for use at a later time. Teachers must remember that facts are not like furniture at all; they are more like dry ice, disappearing at room temperature. Wineburg also stated that "the problem with students is not that they don't know enough about history. The problem is that they don't know what history is in the first place" (Wineburg, 1992). Teachers are doing an incredible disservice to the students when continuing to teach in the traditional ways in which they were taught just because that is the way it was done (Lortie, 1975). Students need to learn in a more engaging and authentic manner that mirrors the procedures utilized by those in the field. Last time I checked, when historians are conducting authentic research, they do not read chapters, answer questions at the back of the book, and take quizzes.

This book makes an effort at overcoming the persistent boredom and lack of historical knowledge present in our students, by focusing on ways in which history instruction can be improved:

- detailed instruction on the process of historical inquiry;
- developing historical thinking skills;
- instruction on accessing and examining various primary and secondary sources;
- varied and multiple opportunities to engage in authentic historical inquiry;
- utilizing methods of interest to digital natives;
- providing scaffolds and various ancillary materials to enhance learning;
- investigate history close to the learner (physical—local history; intellectually—what piques his or her interest); and
- constructive assessments.

As there is no "cookbook" method to teaching, especially for history instruction, this book has not been constructed to show exactly how history should be taught, in a lockstep manner, but rather is intended to be a resource for providing ideas and a spark for bringing history to life for students and teachers in K-16 classrooms.

CHAPTER 2

TEACHING HISTORY LITERATURE

Researchers in education consistently argue that instruction must begin by activating and then building upon students' prior knowledge (R. C. Anderson, 1984; Levstik & Barton, 1997; Salinas, Fraquiz, & Guberman, 2006). History students must be given an opportunity to develop their own understanding; thus, teachers should directly address the knowledge that students bring with them into their classroom and build upon it whenever possible. In order for students to learn, the content to be learned must be linked to the students' previous experiences, understandings, or prior knowledge, as children search for meaning through patterning (Caine & Caine, 1997). Glaser and Resnick (1991) defined prior knowledge as "the preconceptions and mental models they (the students) derive from ordinary experience and bring with them to the classroom" (p. 2). The knowledge that people gain is organized into structures known as schemata or schema (Martorella, 1998a; Slavin, 1997).

A schema is a mental structure that represents a set of information that has been organized together (Howard, 1987). Schemata theory posits that the form and content of all new knowledge encountered by students is shaped by prior knowledge and the information that easily fits within a schema is more readily understood, learned, and retained than information that clashes with an existing schema (Anderson, 1984; Martorella, 1998a; Slavin, 1997). The collections of schemata comprise the cache of prior knowledge that is brought into each new knowledge acquisition task by an individual (Martorella, 1998a).

From the field of developmental psychology, one sees that learning is not passive; people need to compare and contrast new knowledge gained with what they already know (Piaget, 1952). Unfortunately, not much attention is given to prior knowledge in textbooks and other materials being used in history classrooms (Levstik & Barton, 1997; Villano, 2005). Research indicates that when students are not allowed to link new information to an existing schema, students learn very little and that which has been acquired is very superficial (American Psychological Association, 1997; Levstik & Barton, 1997; Rumelhart, 1980; Villano, 2005). People learn most effectively when learning is active, goal directed, and personally relevant (American Psychological Association, 1997); in addition, activating personally relevant background knowledge is known to increase student comprehension and retention (Christen & Murphy, 1991). Christen and Murphy (1991) maintained that:

> We know that prior knowledge is an important step in the learning process. It is a major factor in comprehension: that is, making sense of our learning experiences. Brain-based research confirms the fact that the learning environment needs to provide a setting that incorporates stability and familiarity. It should be able to satisfy the mind's enormous curiosity and hunger for discovery, challenge, and novelty. Creating an opportunity to challenge our students to call on their collective experiences (prior knowledge) is essential. Through this process we move students from memorizing information to meaningful learning and begin the journey of connecting learning events rather than remembering bits and pieces. Prior knowledge is an essential element in this quest for making meaning. (p. 3)

TRANSFER OF KNOWLEDGE

Research on how people learn and how knowledge is transferred has uncovered key principles for structuring learning experiences that enable learners to use what they have learned previously in new situations (Bransford, 2000; National Research Council, Donovan, & Bransford, 2005). A significant finding in the learning and transfer literature is that the organization of information into a conceptual framework allows for greater "transfer" of knowledge; that is, it allows students to apply knowledge learned in new situations and to learn related information more quickly. Bransford (2000) noted that the student "who has learned geographical information from the Americas in a conceptual framework approaches the task of learning the geography of another part of the globe with questions, ideas, and expectations that help guide acquisition of the new information"

(p. 17). Bransford (2000) found that an individual's ability to transfer what was learned depends upon a number of factors:

- People must achieve a threshold of initial learning that is sufficient to support transfer.
- Spending a lot of time ("time on task") in and of itself is not sufficient to ensure effective learning. Most important is how people use their time while learning.
- Learning with understanding is more likely to promote transfer than simply memorizing information from a text or a lecture.
- Knowledge that is taught in a variety of contexts is more likely to support flexible transfer than knowledge that is taught in a single context.
- Students develop flexible understanding of when, where, why, and how to use their knowledge to solve new problems if they learn how to extract underlying themes and principles from their learning exercises.
- Transfer of learning is an active process. Learning and transfer should not be evaluated by "one shot" tests of transfer.
- All learning involves transfer from previous experiences. Even initial learning involves transfer that is based on previous experiences and prior knowledge.
- Sometimes the knowledge that people bring to a new situation impedes subsequent learning because it guides thinking in the wrong directions (pp. 235-237).

The most effective learning can occur when the learner is able to transport what was learned to various and diverse new situations. It is not enough for history teachers to know that subject-matter information needs to be tied to related concepts, if students are to gain a deep understanding and the ability to transfer their learning to future situations. The teacher must recognize the particular concepts that are most relevant for the subject matter that he or she teaches and obtain curriculum materials that support the effort to link information with concepts.

HISTORICAL THINKING AND INQUIRY IN THE CLASSROOM

Researchers increasingly have examined the concept of historical thinking in the K-16 classroom (Drake & Brown, 2003; Hartzler-Miller, 2001; Levstik, 1997; Levstik & Barton, 2005; National Center for History in the Schools, 1996; Tally & Goldenberg, 2005; VanSledright, 2004; Wineburg,

2001, 2010). This approach refers to the idea of allowing students to think like historians by engaging them in the act of "doing history" (Levstik, 1997; Levstik & Barton, 2005; Wineburg, 2001). It is essential that history teachers find ways to allow their students to develop their historical thinking skills and engage them in authentic historical inquiry. More and more, there is an emphasis, within national and state standards, that students be taught historical thinking skills. For example, the 1996 National Standards for History defined history as "a process of reasoning based on evidence from the past" that "must be grounded in the careful gathering, weighing and sifting of factual information such as names, dates, places, ideas, and events" (p. 49). The 1994 National Council for the Social Studies standards stated that a well-designed social studies curriculum will help each learner to construct a blend of views of the human condition. The National Council for the Social Studies maintained that students should learn how to build a personal perspective that allows them to investigate emerging events and persistent or recurring issues and consider implications for themselves, their family, and the national and world community. Researchers argue that educating students through the use of historical thinking fosters important skills, including critical thinking. History students need to be encouraged to learn how to make their own choices after weighing a variety of components, including personal expectations, positive and negative aspects of a situation, responsibilities and expectations, and results of those choices for themselves and others.

History, as it is taught in many schools, too often ignores an essential element of historical thinking by teaching history in a singular form of what happened in the past, void of interpretation (Levstik, 1997). Levstik (1997) contended that American culture presents historical issues as a dichotomous battle between those who are right and wrong or the winners and the losers; she argues that it is essential that history be taught in a way that is contrary to this belief. Other researchers concur and argue that a more effective and engaging method of teaching history allows children to consider multiple perspectives and conduct historical inquiry.

Wineburg (2001) noted that historical thinking is not a natural process and is not something that children attain easily or automatically. Wineburg asserted that its achievement:

> actually goes against the grain of how we ordinarily think, one of the reasons why it is much easier to learn names, dates, and stories than it is to change the basic mental structures we use to grasp the meaning of the past. (p. 7)

Mature historical thinking allows individuals to "go beyond our own image, to go beyond our brief life, and to go beyond the fleeting moment in human history into which we have been born" (Wineburg, 2001, p. 24), and allowing students an opportunity to "know others, whether they live on the other side of the tracks or the other side of the millennium, requires the education of our sensibilities. This is what history, when taught well, gives us practice doing" (pp. 23-24).

Despite the sophisticated nature of historical thinking, research on how students learn history and how it has been taught clearly demonstrates that students, beginning in the earliest of grades, are capable of "doing history" and engaging in historical thinking (Levstik & Barton, 1997; VanSledright, 2002). For example, Booth (1980) argued that history is an adductive process in which children as young as the age of four were able to ask openended questions about historical events and could construct productive answers. It has been found that children, at the youngest ages, are capable of making basic distinctions in historical time (Barton & Levstik, 1996; Brophy & VanSledright, 1997). Barton (1997) found that children in kindergarten were able to determine differences between the present day and events in the past. According to Barton, when children are given the opportunity to learn about the past from familiar sources such as family members, visual images, and tangible objects, they understand history more clearly than when the focus is upon institutional developments. By the time that students have reached the third grade, they are able to distinguish between different time periods, and around the time that students reach the fifth grade, they are able to extensively connect particular dates with specific background knowledge (Barton, 1996; Barton & Levstik, 1996). Clearly, authentic history instruction should and must begin at the earliest possible age; there is no benefit in delaying it (Downey & Levstik, 1988).

DISCIPLINED/HISTORICAL INQUIRY

If children are expected to attribute meaning and to understand how the history that they read in texts, magazines, and books was created and constructed, they must go into the field and authentically create history in a manner similar to that of a professional historian. Researchers refer to this authentic investigation as disciplined inquiry, or historical inquiry (Avery, 2000; Levstik & Barton, 1997; Scheurman & Newmann, 1998). Disciplined inquiry can be thought of as the investigation of personally relevant and intriguing questions in authentic ways. As students conduct historical inquiry, the related instruction should explicitly focus on helping students to weigh historical evidence, examine biases, synthesize information, and reach conclusions so that students understand that the accounts they read are subjective and are the creation of an author who has biases, motives, and beliefs (Barton, 1997). Through historical inquiry, students learn that the accounts that they read are subjective and are created by a person with their own motives and beliefs. By constructing a historical narrative through their own authentic investigation, students can gain a better understanding that there are various viewpoints to each historical event and that no one account is all encompassing.

Historical inquiry also allows authentic intellectual achievement. Scheurman and Newmann (1998) described three criteria for the acquisition of authentic intellectual achievement in history classrooms. First, they noted that authentic intellectual achievement consists of more than the ability to perform well on academic standardized tests. It should involve the application of student knowledge to questions and issues within a specific domain. Second, students must be allowed to build upon prior knowledge, as the simple reproduction of facts does not involve the student in authentic intellectual achievement since it does not allow the student to engage in the thoughtful application of knowledge. Third, they felt that for knowledge construction to be powerful, it must be based on a foundation of disciplined inquiry. Disciplined inquiry must allow the learner to build a "command of the facts, vocabulary, concepts, and theories used in a domain" and "an in-depth understanding of particular problems in the field of study and the ability to express that understanding in ways acceptable to experts" (Scheurman & Newmann, 1998, p. 24).

Unfortunately, the history curriculum is rarely organized in a way that allows students to engage in the kinds of inquiry and communication that are practiced by the members of a particular profession or citizens of a productive society. Creating curriculum designed around a disciplined inquiry model presupposes an understanding of novice-expert differences. The expert would have a better understanding of the key concepts in their field and a more developed understanding of when and how to apply those concepts (Chi, 1976; Sternberg & Horvath, 1995). Students are often allowed to acquire facts without understanding the underpinning concept or even having an idea of its meaning. When a student is asked to regurgitate information such as a date, a capital of a country, or a historical figure's name, it is an all or nothing endeavor. All too often, history is thought of as the memorization of facts, the reading of chapters, and the answering of questions at the end of the chapter or back of the book. It is vital that students are given the opportunity to authentically acquire knowledge through investigations that are meaningful to them and set within a realistic context. When students rush through the acquisition of facts, the best that they can hope for is to retain bits and pieces and maybe have the opportunity to revisit the content at another time in another grade. When students "do" history rather than memorize names, dates, and events, they achieve authentic intellectual achievement. Doing history and engaging in historical inquiry allows discussion of differing points of view. If a teacher presents only selected points of view to be addressed or gives unequal time to alternative points of view, the teacher interferes with the students' ability to authentically learn the material in a personalized and meaningful manner (Lockwood, 1996).

Allowing students opportunities to conduct authentic historical inquiry represents a form of purposeful learning. Dewey (1933) stated that people learn best when they seek answers to questions that matter to them. Children need to learn how to use inquiry or "the process of asking meaningful questions, finding information, drawing conclusions, and reflecting on possible solutions" (Levstik & Barton, 1997) when acquiring history content. Purposeful learning takes place in a sociocultural context, as it is the larger setting that determines what knowledge is worth obtaining, how to get it, and how it should be used (Lave & Wenger, 1991; Resnick, 1987; Rogoff, 1990; Vygotsky, 1978). Avery (2000) noted:

> One of the primary reasons for the low quality of student achievement was the low quality of the tasks or assignments given to students. If students are to produce authentic work, we need to give them the opportunity to do so through authentic assessments, and the support to do so through authentic instruction. (p. 1)

In order for students to be involved in meaningful learning, they must understand the "nature and purpose of that subject—the diverse ways of thinking and acting mathematically, historically, or scientifically in our society" (Levstik & Barton, 1997). Teachers rarely expect their students to engage in authentic inquiry, as textbooks or the curriculum guides determine the content covered rather than allowing the pursuit of meaningful knowledge. Students must be allowed the opportunity to ask and answer questions important to them so that they have the chance to learn through authentic experiences and better understand the roles of real historians (Avery, 2000). The curriculum should be built upon students' prior knowledge in order to properly learn the content and have the greatest opportunity for enduring comprehension.

While allowing students to construct history, it is vital that teachers provide proper scaffolding for the learning process. Students cannot conduct authentic historical inquiry after a brief introduction and asked to write a report on a history related topic. Calder (2006) describes a typical failure by many, when trying to incorporate authentic historical inquiry into history instruction:

> In my early attempts to have students work with primary documents, my efforts misfired because I did not realize how much scaffolding it takes for students to learn the unfamiliar, even off-putting habits of mind historians can take for granted. I thought it would be enough if students watched me

model historical thinking in class, but this assumption proved to be terribly wrong. Students need models, but it is routines that form habits. (p. 1369)

History teachers must begin by working collaboratively with students to "uncover" history (Wiggins & McTighe, 2001) and collectively asking "what is the evidence or reason for believing" what was read in the textbook and other sources that are encountered (Calder, 2006). Working together to deconstruct and construct historical narratives allows students to begin to understand that history is not a clear-cut, definitive story, with a series of "facts" strung together. Calder (2006) suggests that teachers ensure that students are competent in six historical cognitive habits prior moving to independent opportunities to conduct authentic historical inquiry. These habits include: questioning, connecting, sourcing, making inferences, considering alternate perspectives, and recognizing limits to one's knowledge (p. 1364). Similarly, Wineburg (2010) urges that students use specific strategies for reading historical documents, which include: sourcing, contextualizing, close reading, using background knowledge, reading the silences, and corroborating (p. 3). Additionally, Hicks, Doolittle, and Ewing (2004) suggest the utilization of their SCIM-C strategy, which focuses on five broad phases: summarizing, contextualizing, inferring, monitoring, and corroborating. I would suggest a combination, with modifications, of these:

1. *Create authentic questions:* Students must have opportunities to ask questions of personal interest.
2. *Utilize a variety of sources:* A variety of sources (i.e., published documents, unpublished documents, oral histories, visual documents, artifacts, etc.) should be sought to answer the question posed.
3. *Examine the sources:* Each source must be examined to determine who constructed it and why.
4. *Determine the context:* Context for the document is vital. A document taken out of context can lead to invalid conclusions.
5. *Read the sources:* Sources should be read closely and efforts should be made to "read between the lines."
6. *Consider alternative perspectives:* Multiple alternative perspectives must be considered. Finding just the polar extremes is not sufficient.
7. *Corroborate the sources:* Corroborating sources need to be found.
8. *Construct narratives:* Opportunities should be presented where students have a chance to construct historical narratives utilizing the spectrum of sources, while noting where gaps in the sources or the author's knowledge exist.

CHAPTER 3

DEVELOPING HISTORICAL THINKING SKILLS

As any history educator knows, history is, far too often, seen as boring and is typically rated as the least favorite subject of K-16 students (J. Allen, 1994; Black & Blake, 2001; Jensen, 2001; Zhao & Hoge, 2005). However, at the same time, many of the top grossing films released each year contain historical plots and historical elements. In addition, scores of video games, many of which are best sellers, have themes based on significant social and historical events. Given the popularity of history outside of the classroom, why is it so unpopular within the classroom?

Much of the distaste for history, in the K-16 classroom, stems from the way in which it is taught. The traditional approach, teaching history as series of lectures, textbook reading, note memorizing, and test taking, is not only boring to students (Fertig, 2005; Hicks, Carroll, Doolittle, Lee, & Oliver, 2004), but it is also ineffective in garnering real historical learning (Scheuerell, 2007). In the history classroom, students must be encouraged to think historically, have multiple opportunities to engage in authentic learning (Levstik & Barton, 2005; O'Brien & White, 2006; Okolo, Ferretti, & MacArthur, 2007; White, O'Brien, Hileman, Mortensen, & Smith, 2006), and think critically (Fuchs, 2006; Goldenberg & Tally, 2005; National Council for the Social Studies, NCSS, 2008). In order to have opportunities to think critically, students should take part in "the kind of thinking involved in solving problems, formulating inferences, calculating

Preserving History: The Construction of History in the K-16 Classroom
pp. 15–28
Copyright © 2011 by Information Age Publishing
All rights of reproduction in any form reserved.

likelihoods, and making decisions" (Halpern, 2007, p. 6). Furthermore, a foundation for thinking critically and historically must be developed as early as possible. A strong foundation for critical and historical thinking will make students more perceptive and discriminating consumers when faced with lectures, note taking, textbook reading, and other didactic modes of instruction in future history classrooms. What is more, students will be able to build upon this foundation beyond the K-16 classrooms (Facione, 2004). However, the dual skills of critical and historical thinking must be consciously taught and learned, as they do not develop in isolation on their own (Rudd, 2007; Schuster, 2008).

Historians conventionally have used primary sources, such as clothing, letters, photographs, census records, maps, and manuscripts, as evidence when conducting historical inquiries (Barton, 1997, 2001; Levstik & Barton, 2005; Library of Congress, 2003). Traditionally, primary sources are rarely used in history classrooms, although students beginning in the earliest of grades enjoy working with primary sources, can critically analyze them, and have been found to utilize them in the creation of historical narratives (Barton, 1997). The minimal use of primary sources in history classroom has been due, in the past, primarily to the lack of availability of primary sources and time that educators have to locate primary sources. The lack of use can also be attributed to several other factors: (a) a student's lack of understanding as to why it is important to understand how history is interpreted (Barton, 1996; Downey & Levstik, 1991; Morris, Morgan-Fleming, & Janisch, 2001), (b) epistemological assumptions about the nature of knowledge and how it is generated (Lee, 1998; VanSledright, 1998, 2002), (c) a lack of understanding about historical thinking processes (Bohan & Davis, 1998; Thornton & Vukelich, 1988; Yeager & Davis, 1994), and (d) a lack of deep content knowledge or perceptions toward teaching historical content for the average history teacher, especially in the elementary grades (Gillaspie & Davis, 1997-1998; Goodman & Adler, 1985).

What follows here is a description of lessons within a mini-unit created to assist students in the development of a foundation for historical and critical thinking. The lessons are aimed at assisting students to think historically, giving students opportunities to analyze multiple perspectives, allowing students to discover the necessity of using multiple sources when conducting research, and guiding students to learn how to construct historical narratives through the creation of a digital historical biography.

WHAT IS A HISTORIAN AND WHAT ARE PRIMARY SOURCES?

In the first portion of this mini-unit, the idea is to allow students to gain a better appreciation for the role of a historian and the sources utilized during the construction of historical narratives. Prior to the students entering the classroom, write the words "historian" and "primary sources" across the board. Ask the students to define these two terms using their own words or by drawing pictures. After approximately 2 minutes, ask the students, "What is a historian?" Use this discussion as a jumping off point to beginning the process of engaging students in authentic historical inquiry. Once students have a better understanding of what it is that a historian is and does, they will be more successful in replicating steps similar to those of a historian.

Next, the students should be asked to think about what primary sources are; typical student responses might be "sources we use," "sources we get," "sources used long ago," or "sources that historians need." As these are common incomplete or misunderstandings when discussing the work of historians with novice historical thinkers, one way to begin the process of understanding these terms is by taking students on a "mindwalk" (Library of Congress, 2002). For this mindwalk, students are asked to recall all of the activities in which they were involved during the previous 24 hours. Then, the students are prompted to provide any evidence that proves they existed during the last 24 hours. A good example scenario for students to discuss is the act of purchasing and pumping gasoline at a service station. The actions involved in getting gas are well known by most students, but few have consciously thought about all the potential evidence left behind when getting gas (i.e., paper and electronic receipts, video surveillance, garbage discarded, purchasing of merchandise inside, discussions with individuals who could attest to conversations, etc.). After several minutes, the students are asked to reveal some of the evidence proving their existence. You may expect to receive an answer such as, "my dad saw me doing my homework yesterday at my house." This student suggested that his dad could vouch for his existence. Another answer might be, "I left my hat at my friend's house yesterday while playing video games." In this case, the hat would be the proof of the student's existence. In order to get past just human interactions, the students might need to be probed in to thinking beyond these interactions, "Are there any answers that do not involve or depend on people as proof of your existence?" To this, you might expect an answer like, "I left a dish in the sink yesterday" as proof of existence, or "I touched a bench and left a fingerprint." The instructor and the students can discuss how these answers tell a story about a past event or place and are "primary sources."

The discussion about primary sources can segue into an activity where students are asked to examine a set of different primary sources about a particular subject to be studied, like the Boston Massacre. The students can focus on the artifact set as a whole and determine why each item would be included or why each source was relevant to the Boston Massacre. While investigating the artifacts, the students can begin to discover,

18 *Preserving History: The Construction of History in the K-16 Classroom*

through instruction and open discourse, how primary sources are the tools that historians use to tell a story. To help further convey this point, an example featuring the volcanic eruption at Pompeii, Italy in AD 79, or other historical site, can be used. The instructor can explain that, without the primary sources preserved by the ashes from the eruption of Mount Vesuvius, historians would know much less about human life in Europe over 2,000 years ago and how human life has progressed since. Overall, the mindwalk activity and primary source set investigation generates an excellent interactive discussion about historians and primary sources while also creating a foundation for more mature levels of historical thinking.

With a better idea of the definitions of both historians and primary sources, as a result of the mindwalk, the lesson can be expanded by playing a game of hide-and-seek. Students are asked to look at a projected image related to the content under study; one example of an effective source might be an image of a bread peddler in an Italian immigrant community at the beginning of the twentieth century. In Figure 3.1 the image of the *Italian Bread Peddler* (Byron, c.1900), from the Library of

Figure 3.1. Italian bread peddler.

Congress' American Memory website, is a perfect image for the hide and seek. It shows a food cart in front of a store of some kind. Next to the cart, there is a bicycle. Around the food cart, there are people posing. The students are asked to think about the rules to a game of hide-and-seek. After a discussion of the rules and how they can be used for a game of hide-and-seek with the image, the students are asked to find the best place to hide within this picture. After about a minute, the students are informed that the hunt to find them in the picture has begun. The large bread basket located in the middle of the image is the first location that can be "searched." Those students who chose this hiding place are asked to imagine themselves actually hiding inside the bread basket, to picture themselves in that moment of time in the photo. Questions exploring the human senses (sight, hearing, touch, smell, taste), along with traditional journalistic inquiries (who, what, where, when, and why), are employed with the students as they are asked "What does it smell like?", "What do you feel?", and "Is it fresh bread?". When asked what they were able to hear, various student answers might include discussions about the creaking of the wheels on the food cart and people talking. Regarding the possible languages the people in the photo may have spoken, the students should be asked, "What language or languages do you hear?" or "Is this a language you recognize?". To this, one student might reply, "English," while another might say "Spanish" or "Italian." This open flow of thoughts can help to facilitate a discussion as to how this photo might not be one of American origin or of individuals native to this country and about how a historian might go about researching this image further. Hiding places are examined until all of the students are found and all of the important details of the photo are discussed. The lesson can be capped off by explaining to the students that what they just engaged in, the envisioning of what things were like in historical photos by picturing themselves in the moment of the photo, is very similar to what historians do with these sorts of primary sources.

ANALYZING PRIMARY SOURCES

Keeping with the same lesson theme, another picture (see Figure 3.2), an image of an American Civil War era mortar (Knox, 1864), is an effective image to introduce. It should be explained to the students that a historian, who wants to know more about this picture, would ask questions about it and critically analyze the elements within the image. An inquiry activity can be initiated by asking the students if the image that they were viewing was an old or new picture. The students often will believe it to be old, because the picture is in black and white, the clothes the people were

Figure 3.2. American Civil War era mortar.

wearing in the picture are of a different style from that of a contemporary one, and there is an antiquated looking "war cannon" in the picture. It should then revealed that the picture is from 1864, at the time of the American Civil War. In order to delve more deeply into this image, the students should be informed that they will be looking at it section by section (Hines & Day, 2002). The instructor should be sure that sections of the picture are covered so that only the top third of it is visible. The students then are asked, based on what they can see on the uncovered part of the photo, what time of year or what season it might be. At first, students may not know where to begin their investigation for this section of the image, so the instructor can suggest that they begin by looking at the trees. The students can be asked, "Based on how the trees look, can you figure out what time of year it is?" The students then make an educated guess as to what time of year it is in the picture and may respond with ideas such as "I think the trees looked bare, so fall or winter."

Next, the way the photo looks can be changed by covering up everything except for one particular person in the photo. The students should be instructed to think about how the man looks and can be asked again, "What time of the year is it in the photo?" The students should look at the man and, based on his appearance, start guessing. Many students may guess spring or summer, because the man appears to be sweating in the picture and has the sleeves on his shirt rolled up. Thus, the students' guesses may change as they viewed the photo in different parts and learn additional information. Next, the students can be asked, based on looking only at this particular person in the photo, what time of the day they think it was when the photo was taken. One student might notice the person in the photo is squinting (or the person's face looks bright with light) and guess that the photo might have been taken in the early afternoon. Another might point out the shadow of the person and its length. Given the position of the person's shadow, students guess what time of day it is in the photo.

After the students finish determining the time of day, the photo can be rearranged to emphasize the "antiquated looking" mortar. The students should be asked as to what, in their minds, are the main elements that stick out in regards to this mortar. Although various answers may be given, most of the students say that the mortar looks old, fat, and short. One student might point out that there are steps leading up to the cannon. The instructor could then prompt with a question about the purpose of these steps. One student might believe that the steps are there to help people get to the cannon. Another might believe the steps are there so people can have access to clean the cannon. Finally, portions of the photo should be covered up, one final time, so that the students focus only on the people standing next to the mortar. The students can be asked, "What do you think these people do?" Students may suggest that the people are soldiers and part of an army because the photo was taken during the American Civil War. The fact that the people are standing next to a mortar, a weapon commonly used in nineteenth century warfare, also influences the students' notion that the people are soldiers.

This activity can, once again, assist the students in understanding the role of an historian and how sources influence the construction of historical narratives. Thus, this lesson can be concluded by asking the students, "How would we change the definitions of historian and primary sources, knowing what we know now?" Working democratically, with the students as a whole class, the new definition for "historian" might became something like "someone who looks at pictures to learn about history"; the new class definition for "primary sources" might be altered to read "things used to prove that something exists and that gives us details or provides evidence about the past." As the lesson closes, a final effort to authentically relate the content of the lesson to students can be made by asking them to compare the role of the historian to certain television shows with investigative formats. The students can be asked to think about some of these shows and share examples with the class. They might suggest that, in shows like *Law and Order*, *CSI*, *Blue's Clues*, and even *Scooby Doo*, characters conduct investigations and analyze evidence, which are tasks similar to that of the historian. One student, with whom I was working, began by being completely confused as to the role of historians and primary sources. He summed everything up by saying that both the characters in the aforementioned television shows and historians "look for and investigate evidence to develop facts and stories about the past."

MULTIPLE PERSPECTIVES OF HISTORICAL EVENTS

The focus of the following lesson is to open students' minds to different perspectives of historical events and to think more critically about information and sources with which they have been presented. To do this, the lesson begins with showing the students a sheet of construction paper. On one side of the sheet, the letter "I" is written. On the other side of the sheet, the letter "T" is written. The students are asked to look at the paper and to think about what they see. Only one part of the class can see the I, while another segment of the class can only see the T. When asked what they see, almost half of the class says they see the I. Predictably, approximately 50% of the class says they see the T. Several students indicate that they see the side of the construction paper or portions of both letters. The point of the activity is that, from different standpoints, people see things differently. One person might see an I, but another one might see a T. The students are told that this is true when historians retell what has happened during historical time periods, and thus, they need to keep that in mind whenever reading historical accounts.

To build upon this thought, the students are read *The True Story of the 3 Little Pigs* (Scieszka, 1995). The students are asked to keep in mind the earlier demonstration about perspectives while listening to the story. Basically, *The True Story of the 3 Little Pigs* offers an alternative perspective to the traditional tale of *The Three Little Pigs*. The story is told from the wolf's point of view. When the story is completed, the students are asked, while referring back to the I and T exercise, "How does this different version of *The Three Little Pigs* relate to history?" A typical student might answer, "Well, the wolf has one side to the story, and the reporters and pigs have another side to the story." While wrapping up this part of the lesson, the students are told that, in regards to history, many people who were actually in attendance during a historical event will have their own account of the event, and thus, multiple thoughts about one historical event will be present. When asked if every rendition of every historical event will be the

Developing Historical Thinking Skills 23

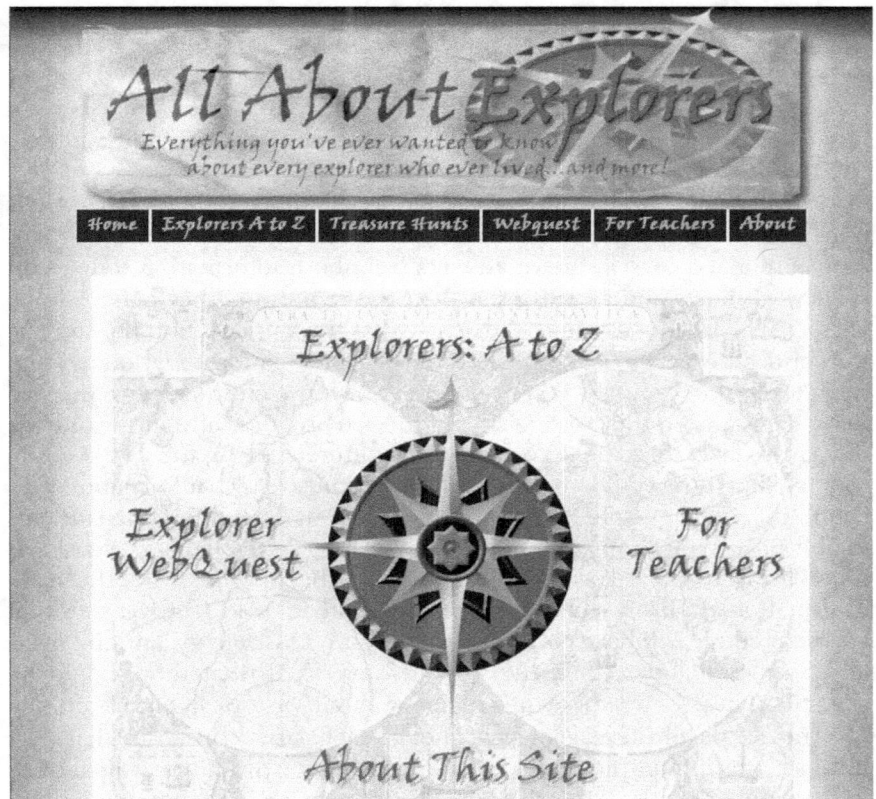

Figure 3.3. All About Explorer website.

same, the students all agree that they will differ, that every historical event will be remembered or interpreted differently.

For the third part of this lesson, the students engage in an activity called the *Explorer Treasure Hunt* (Aungst & Zucker, 2007). With this activity, the students are first instructed to go to the All About Explorers website (www.allaboutexplorers.com). Then, the students, in small groups, are given an explorer to research from the website and a guiding worksheet. To aid the students in their research, they are given access, through the All About Explorers website, to two other websites with information on their assigned explorer. Then, the students are asked, based on the information from their two website sources, to answer three questions on the worksheet about their explorer. The questions assigned to the student researching Juan Ponce de Leon are: When and where was Juan Ponce de

Leon born?; What official position did de Leon hold in Puerto Rico?; and Where was de Leon buried? The catch with this assignment is that the two website sources the students are using have differing information about their explorer. Some information, therefore, might not be correct. In other words, the information was created from authors with different perspectives or who are conveying misinformation.

As the students begin to work on the assignment, they realize their website sources tell two different stories about their explorers. The students are asked to write down answers from both information sources on their worksheets and to put a star next to the answers they believe to be correct. The final question of the activity has the students find the similarities and differences between the differing information they found from their two online sources. When students finish the entire activity, the primary focus was on the last question of the activity. Typically, most students quickly realize that the information is different from the two website sources, but how could they tell what was the correct information and from where it originated? When this question has been offered to students in the past, typical answers ranged from "the better looking website is more likely to have correct information;" "the websites with the most information are likely to have the correct sources;" and "the websites that looked credible will have correct information." This activity, and the overall lesson, concludes when the students are asked what they should do when looking for credible information about historical events on the Internet. Typically, the class, as a whole, reaches the consensus that they must search in multiple places to find information and then evaluate this information carefully. After this activity, students begin to understand that they can use historical information in confidence only after multiple perspectives have been considered and evaluated critically.

PERSPECTIVES

One of the most prevalent strands running through history curriculum is *perspective*: historical, personal, and cultural. Historical perspective must be addressed in the history classroom. Students can start to see perspectives through the participation in *artifact bag* activities and document-based questioning, during which students are given an opportunity to view various primary sources and discuss each item's relevance to the topic of discovery. For example, World War II on the American home front can be utilized as the topics for this activity. This topic is a good one, as the Second World War is generally considered a meaningful historical event; Barton (1997) indicated that *effective* primary source investigations, conducted early in the historical inquiry learning process, should be on meaningful historic events. World War II artifact bags can consist of ration coupons, images and posters, chewing gum, advertisements, metal lipstick tubes, nylon stockings, and other items important to the investigation of the American home front. This is an important activity, as the process of comparing and contrasting primary source artifacts is a basic skill of historical inquiry. Students should be given opportunities to investigate and analyze various primary sources and compare their findings with classmates to gain a better understanding of the historical inquiry process (Barton, 2001).

Several additional digital sources can be downloaded and investigated with the students to practice and better understand the process of thinking like a historian: create authentic questions, utilize a variety of sources, examine the sources, determine the context, read the sources, consider alternative perspectives, corroborate the sources, and construct narratives. These include portions of documentary movies on Japanese Internment camps produced by the U.S. War Relocation Authority (*Challenge to Democracy*) and the U.S. Office of War Information (*Japanese Relocation*) and primary sources from the Library of Congress (Japanese American Internment During World War II Primary Source Set). Materials from the Library of Congress include an *Interview with Marielle Tsukamoto: A Firsthand Account of Japanese Internment,* Civilian Exclusion Order Number 33, and Executive Order 9066. These two orders mandated the internment of Japanese Americans in the United States during the Second World War (see Figure 3.4). Additionally, poems written by internees can be located online and read to the students, as well as children's literature such as *Baseball Saved Us* (Mochizuki, 1995).

Since, students beginning as early as the elementary grades have the ability to conduct historical inquiries and evaluate primary sources (Barton, 1997, 2001; Levstik & Barton, 1994, 2005), there is a need for teachers, at all levels, to correctly model the use of digital primary sources and historical inquiry based assignments in their classrooms, as this might be the only opportunity students have to witness and experience authentic historical inquiry and methods for learning about history that utilize primary sources. Levstik and Barton (1994) found that history instruction should "focus upon helping students refine and extend the knowledge they have gained about history" (pp. 33-34), and Barton (1997) posited that "students need systematic exposure to the collection and evaluation of historical evidence" (p. 423). Educators need to carefully examine the practices used in their history classrooms, as students will not have this opportunity if proper techniques are not provided within this arena (Seixas, 1998). When conscious efforts to utilize these techniques in history instruction are not made, unfortunately, teachers may fall back upon the practices that were used during their own K-16 schooling. This

26 *Preserving History: The Construction of History in the K-16 Classroom*

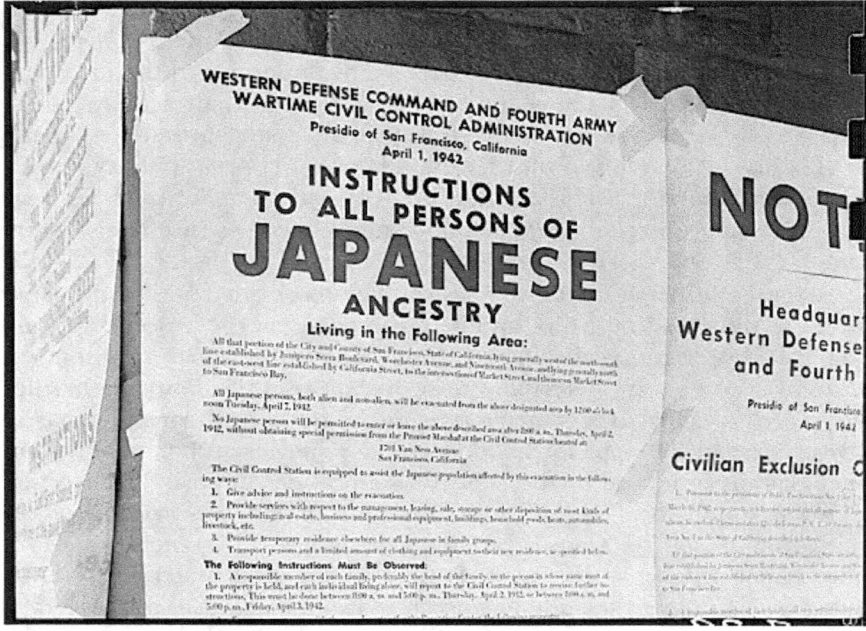

Figure 3.1. Orders mandating the internment of Japanese Americans.

"apprenticeship of observation" (Lortie, 1975) is likely the worst scenario possible.

The current literature is replete with documentation of the narrowing and marginalization of history curriculum and instruction (Allen, 1994; Black & Blake, 2001; Jensen, 2001; Leming, Ellington, & Schug, 2006; Van Fossen, 2005; Vogler & Virtue, 2007; Zhao & Hoge, 2005). Within my context of working in schools, I have recognized this *present absence* (Grumet, 1988) of history instruction. However, I also have worked collaboratively with history teachers who continue to find space to teach in robust and meaningful ways: using primary sources to facilitate historical thinking and inquiry, integrating technology into their curriculum, and going beyond the prescribed textbooks in order to have students engage more authentically in the learning of history.

ENGAGING IN AN AUTHENTIC HISTORICAL ASSESSMENT ACTIVITY

The final activity, within this historical thinking module, is to allow students an opportunity to research a historical figure of their choice. It is clearly stated that the students must, when conducting their research, put into practice the critical thinking, historical thinking, and historical inquiry skills they learned from the above lessons. Therefore, the aforementioned activities centered on primary source analysis and multiple historical perspectives serve as excellent preparatory lessons for this final activity.

For their research, the students utilize a variety of web resources and a minimum of two print sources. Having students gather several sources for their research is a key component in making this assessment activity authentic. Through the process of gathering multiple historical sources, students are put in the position of the social scientist or historian by having them apply the same skills as these professionals would on a daily basis (Gulikers, Bastiaens, & Kirschner, 2004). After the bulk of their research is gathered, the students creat digital movies, using Microsoft Movie Maker, about their historical figures. Movie Maker has used only out of convenience, as other digital video editing software packages work just as well or better. Before the creation of the movies, the students have to synthesize their research into a historical narrative that includes information about the lives and accomplishments of their historical figures. By developing historical narratives, students are again engaging in an authentic activity. Historians depend on narratives to not only convey facts about the past but to also interpret how the past truly was based on factual evidence (Immerwhar, 2008). In making these narratives, students will understand that history is not only a matter of fact gathering, but also of interpretation. Once the narratives are constructed, the students gathered digital pictures of their historical figures and upload them into Movie Maker; the uploaded pictures are then turned into a slideshow. Then, the students record their narratives into their computers to coincide with the slideshows of the historical figures. The historical narratives act as "scripts" for the students to refer to when recording.

A convenient feature of this final activity is its flexibility. Since the final activity is a research project on a historical figure, the entire mini-unit can be easily inserted into almost any section of a school's history curriculum. For example, if an American history class is studying the American Revolution, this final activity can be focused on notable figures of the revolution. If a class is reviewing the Enlightenment period in Europe, this final activity can be geared towards the great Enlightenment philosophers of that period. Even if it is not desirable to use the final activity suggested here, the first two activities, on primary source analysis and multiple historical perspectives, can provide a suitable background for an alternative authentic historical and critical thinking assessment activity. Such alternative activities may include the use of primary sources and multiple historical perspectives.

CONCLUSION

Clearly, the lessons and activities outlined here attempt to get away from the lecture, note taking, and testing ritual that is traditionally synonymous with teaching history. These activities also avoid student interaction with history textbooks, which tend to present history content as stationary and discourage further historical investigation by students (Bain, 2006). However, given the suggestions made, it is not recommended that lecturing, note taking, test taking, and textbook reading be completely eliminated from history instruction. All of these exercises, if planned and implemented properly, can teach students important skills that will allow them to become more critical consumers when encountering these methods of instruction in the future.

Nevertheless, when it comes to teaching students about historical thinking and getting these students to think more critically about the information and sources they encounter, it is highly recommended that history instruction contain activities that stimulate historical inquiry (Goldenberg & Tally, 2005). Employing the lessons and activities delineated here will allow students to develop genuine historical thinking skills. The development of such skills is vital at the earliest possible opportunity, to ensure academic success in the K-16 history classroom. More importantly, students with sound historical thinking skills are, by default, sound critical thinkers (Levstik & Barton, 2005; Martin & Wineburg, 2008; Wineburg, 2001) and critical thinking is a crucial component in the creation of competent citizens for a global, multicultural, and democratic society such as ours (Barton & Levstik, 2004; Paul & Elder, 2000). By enhancing the historical and critical thinking skills of students today, they will be aware of, and prepared for, the academic, civic, and societal challenges that await them in their years ahead (Facione, 2004).

CHAPTER 4

MULTIPLE PRESENTATIONS OF HISTORY

The Battle of Lexington Green

History students need to be encouraged to learn how to make their own choices after weighing a variety of components, including personal expectations, positive and negative aspects of a situation, responsibilities and expectations, and results of those choices for themselves and others. History, as it is taught in many schools, too often ignores an essential element of historical thinking by teaching history as static facts to be learned and in a singular form of what happened in the past, void of interpretation (Hartzler-Miller, 2001; Levstik, 1997). Levstik (1997) contended that American culture presents historical issues as a dichotomous battle between those who are right and wrong or the winners and the losers; she argued that it is essential that history be taught in a way that is contrary to this belief. Other researchers concur and argue that a more effective and engaging method of teaching history allows children to consider multiple perspectives and conduct historical inquiry (Drake & Brown, 2003).

Wineburg (2001) noted that historical thinking is not a natural process and is not something that children attain easily or automatically. Wineburg asserted that its achievement:

actually goes against the grain of how we ordinarily think, one of the reasons why it is much easier to learn names, dates, and stories than it is to change the basic mental structures we use to grasp the meaning of the past. (p. 7)

Mature historical thinking allows individuals to "go beyond our own image, to go beyond our brief life, and to go beyond the fleeting moment in human history into which we have been born" (Wineburg, 2001, p. 24). As students are given opportunities to use "primary source material, contextual clues, empathy and imagination to interpret events, they experience the ways in which authors' backgrounds and values influence historical accounts" (Hartzler-Miller, 2001, p. 676).

Researchers predict that technology use in education is increasing and will continue to do so, particularly given the mandates of state and national standards (International Society for Technology in Education, 2004; Kleiner & Farris, 2002; Newburger, 2001). Technology is the perfect medium to assist educators in an effort to allow students to think and act as historians (Martorella, 1998b; Mason et al., 2000). The World Wide Web (WWW) offers history educators ample opportunities for providing their students inquiry based lessons through data collection and analysis of primary and secondary sources (Milson, 2002) and, most importantly, in ways that the instructor could not do without technology or, at least, in a more efficient manner (Dawson & Harris, 1999). Many educators teaching history content are still relying upon the textbook as their primary source of information for their students (Lee, Doolittle, & Hicks, 2006), and it is also unlikely that these individuals will raise probing questions or create activities that allow the text to come to life (Ravitch, 1998). Thus, preservice teachers must be made aware of how technology, more specifically the WWW, facilitates the acquisition of historical thinking and inquiry skills.

Students must be taught the skills necessary to successfully evaluate online sources for accuracy, authority, and authenticity. Prior to any activity evaluating multiple representations of historical events, time should be spent looking at how one would properly evaluate online historical sources. The Cornell University Library's (2006) Five Criteria for Evaluating Web Pages (http://www.library.cornell.edu/olinuris/ref/research/webcrit.html) and Purdue University Library's Comprehensive Online Research Education Tutorial (http://gemini.lib.purdue.edu/core) offer great resources for assisting educators in evaluating online resources. Without this basic knowledge, evaluating multiple representations, taken from online sources, of historical events would not be as valuable of an endeavor.

Multiple Presentations of History 31

The following activity looks at the way in which the WWW can be utilized to teach a historical event, specifically the Battle of Lexington Green. This process gives students an opportunity to think like historians, by engaging them in authentic historical inquiry. Through a focus on the Battle of Lexington Green, teachers can illustrate the fact that different accounts, of the same historical event, may be portrayed in dissimilar ways and even confuse and include contradictions to other historical accounts and sources, even though there has been over 200 years to come to some consensus. This process allows students to have an opportunity to use various accounts, available on the WWW, to construct their own understanding of a range of aspects of this historical event.

An introductory video, entitled *Road to Revolution* (http://www.cyberbee.com/viewpoints/intro.swf) which is available on the Revolutionary Viewpoints website (http://www.cyberbee.com/viewpoints), is used as a precursor to the investigation of the Battle of Lexington Green. This video provides a brief overview of some of the events leading up to the first shots of the American Revolution, which gives them enough background information to begin their inquiry.

Next, the students are provided with several websites that discuss the events of the Battle of Lexington Green. These sites were some of the first results returned after performing a search through one of the most commonly utilized search engines, a procedure similar to that which might be used by a school-aged student who was asked to investigate information about an historical event. As the students have the opportunity to investigate this list of websites pertaining to the Battle of Lexington Green, they are asked to fill in sections of a question sheet that is provided to them. This sheet includes questions such as: "How many British were present?"; "How many Americans were present?"; and "Who fired first?".

The first web page that is shared with the students is one that is part of a website created for Henderson Island (http://www.geocities.com/mwinthrop/majpit5.html), which is part of the Pitcairn Island group in the south Pacific. This island group was named for the son of Major John Pitcairn, a participant in the Battle of Lexington Green. The creator of this website decided to include information about Major Pitcairn and his involvement in the American Revolution. In this account, it is stated that 77 armed American Militia were present and in formation on the green, while Pitcairn brought 200 well equipped marines with him that morning. It is stated that "it is known that Parker's men did return fire, though it is unlikely that they held their ground for long" (para. 10). This site indicates that after the battle was complete, eight Americans died and 10 more were wounded.

The next site that was shared with the students is that of the Jubilee Newspaper (http://www.jubilee-newspaper.com/lexington_94.htm), which

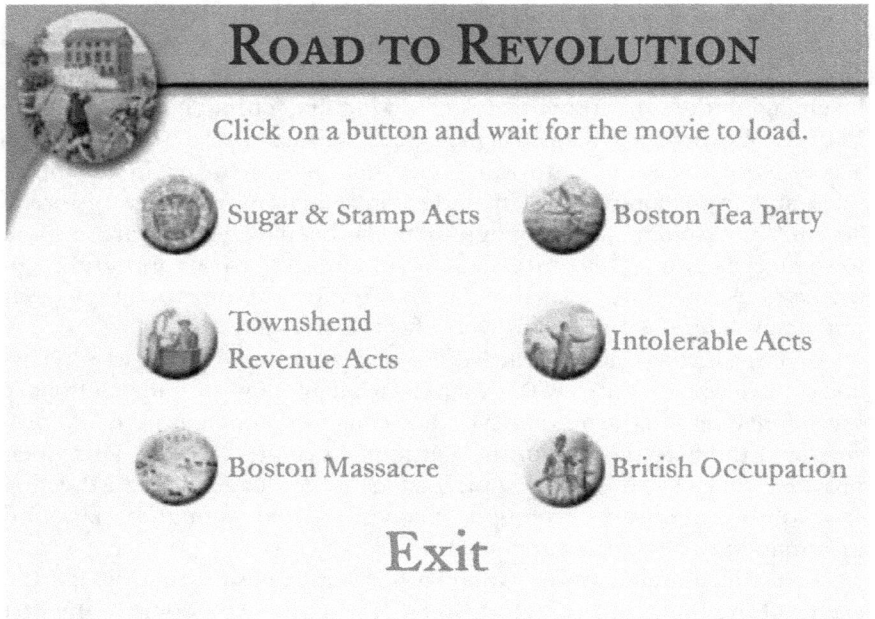

Figure 4.1. Road to Revolution website.

dubs itself as being "The Newspaper of Record for the American Christian Patriot." On this site, there is a section entitled, "The Battle of Lexington: A Day All Patriots Should Remember." This section of the site reports that the battle pitted "a British contingent of 140 grenadiers" (para. 1) versus "70 Patriots of Lexington" (para. 2). The site mentions that after the battle ended "eight brave Patriots fell dead and ten lay wounded on the Lexington Green" (para. 3). When addressing the question of whether the American Militiamen fired, this site notes that "the courageous men of Lexington returned one volley of shot into the British line wounding but one" (para. 3). This is also a good lesson to discuss bias and how language can alter perceptions of how an historical event occurred and the nature of the participants involved.

The third site, Public Bookshelf (http://www.publicbookshelf.com), states on their homepage that the information available on their site is "as is, with all faults." The page provided about the Battle of Lexington Green (http://www.publicbookshelf.com/public_html/Our_Country_vol_2/battlelex_ff.html) is from "Our Country," which was originally published in 1877 as a "Household History for All Readers." This version of the Battle of Lexington Green indicates that "eight hundred British troops marched silently to the foot of the Common," although it does not mention the exact numbers that were involved in the battle. The American leader Captain Parker "found himself at the head of almost seventy men" (para. 5). As the battle neared, Major Pitcairn is thought to have yelled "Disperse, you villains! Lay down your arms! Why don't you disperse, you rebels? Disperse!" (para. 6). The site mentions that at that very moment, the British soldiers fired some random shots over the heads of the Americans, but had no effect. It also indicates that the "Minute-men had scruples about firing, until their own blood had been spilled" and that once "the blood of their comrades had been shed, and as the shrill fife of young Jonathan Harrington set the drum a-beating, the patriots returned the fire with spirit, but not with fatal effect" (para. 7). Eight minutemen died as a result of the skirmish. No British soldier lost his life in this battle, but three of the British were wounded, "with Pitcairn's horse" (para. 7).

The next site that the students have the opportunity to view is from the Department of Military Science at Worcester Polytechnic Institute (http://www.wpi.edu/Academics/Depts/MilSci/Resources/lexcon.html). This site indicates that the British column, consisting of "650-900 troops" (para. 2), arrived at Lexington Green and that Pitcairn ordered the militia "to be surrounded and disarmed" (para. 4). In the end, eight Americans were killed and 10 more were wounded and "so started the first battle in the American Revolutionary War" (para. 5). This version goes on to state that the "British column then advanced to Concord ... This time when shots rang out the Americans were more prepared and fired back in "The Shot Heard Round The World" and so began the American Revolution" (para. 6), which contradicts all of the other sites, and even itself, about where the "The Shot Heard Round the World" occurred.

Through the website "Battle at Lexington Green, 1775: The Start of the American Revolution and the 'shot heard round the world' " (http://www.eyewitnesstohistory.com/lexington.htm), the students are given an opportunity to view a primary source account, a sworn affidavit, that indicates that the Americans never fired upon the British. All of the other accounts they investigate note that the Americans fired upon the British, after being fired upon, except for this primary source. In the words of 23-year-old Sylvanus Wood, one of the Lexington militia present that morning on Lexington Green, "There was not a gun fired by any of Captain Parker's company, within my knowledge. I was so situated that I must have known it, had any thing of the kind taken place before a total dispersion of our company" (para. 9).

By investigating these sources, as well as others, the students find that many different representations of the Battle of Lexington Green exist.

They find that the British contingent numbered anywhere from 140 to 1,300 soldiers and that these British marines faced an American force of somewhere between 39 and 130 militiamen. Also, we learn that eight Americans were killed and 10 wounded, but we are not exactly sure of what Pitcairn yelled, how many British were injured, or if the horse is included in the statistics. Some of the questions that are asked of them have a clear-cut answer, while some answers have great inconsistency between them.

Once the students have had ample opportunity to review the Internet sources, they are asked to look at a group of six paintings interpreting the Battle of Lexington Green from the Revolutionary Viewpoints website (http://www.cyberbee.com/viewpoints). They are asked to gather in small groups so that they may view these while collectively answering questions from a "What Do You See" guide. Together, they go through the three sections of the guide: observation, knowledge, and interpretation. These sections ask the students questions that allow them to describe exactly what they see in each of the paintings, to summarize what they already know about the situation and time period shown and the people and objects that appear, and to discuss the conclusions that can be made from what they are able to see in the images. Last, they are asked to discuss what questions that the images have raised and what are some sources that can be used to find those answers.

Lastly, the students have an opportunity to view a reenactment video of the battle on The Battle of Lexington: Patriot's Day Reenactment 2003 website (http://www.mit.edu/people/endeavor/Battle). The students are asked to think about the data collected about the Battle of Lexington Green from their prior knowledge, the websites reviewed, the historical paintings, and the reenactment video. They discuss similarities and differences between the various resources and decide how the Battle of Lexington Green might have "occurred" and how it might be presented to school aged students. This process helps them to better understand the process of historical inquiry, how historians create historical accounts, and that bias, interpretation, and multiple representations exist in historical narratives.

Recently, teachers, in the state of Florida, were presented with House Bill 7087 that states that American history should be viewed as "factual, not as constructed, shall be viewed as knowable, teachable, and testable" (line 1159-1161). This causes great consternation for all involved in history education. This mindset is most difficult for students in the classroom, as they are confronted with differing interpretations and representations throughout their education and are tested on these "knowable facts."

Multiple Presentations of History   35

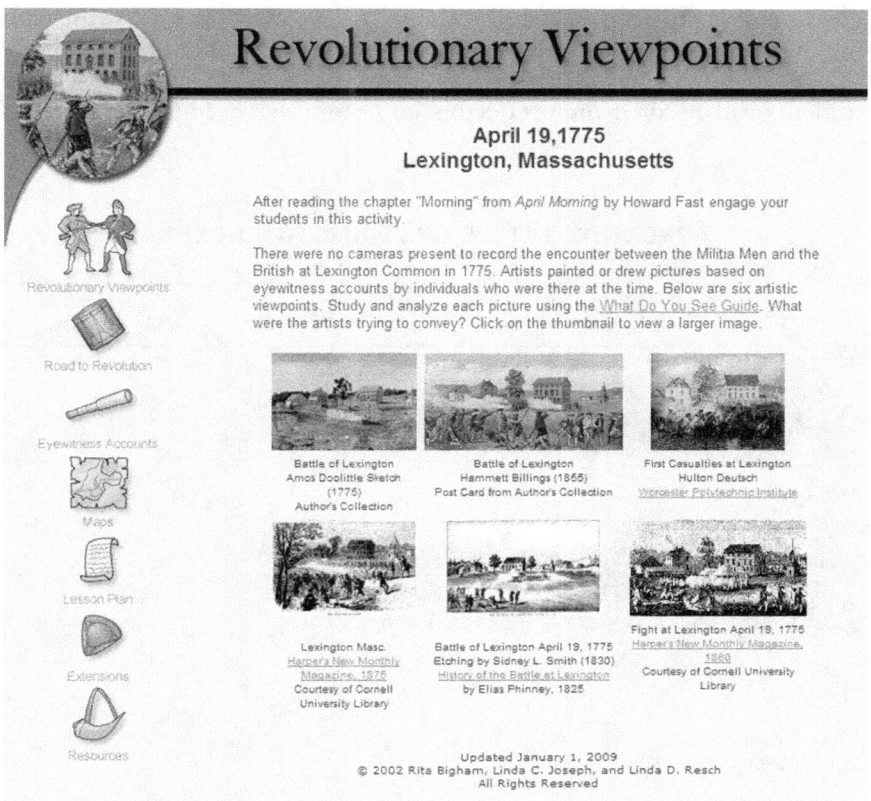

Figure 4.2.   Six paintings interpreting the Battle of Lexington Green from the Revolutionary Viewpoints website.

It is essential that students are provided the skills and knowledge necessary to enable them to conduct effective online historical inquiry. By having an opportunity to evaluate multiple sources of a single historical event, students begin to understand that much of what is told and written about historical events is subject to the interpretation of its author and that varying accounts do exist. This activity also opens an opportunity for further investigation of primary and secondary sources as well as searching for other perspectives, specifically that of the British. This process utilizes the WWW for purposes of allowing preservice teachers the opportunity to understand that multiple representations exist of historical events while allowing them to see the benefit of permitting their future students the opportunity to engage in authentic historical inquiry through the utilization of the resources provided through the WWW. Once empowered with the knowledge and skill base necessary to conduct online research and inquiry based assignments, these students will become more effective and empowered consumers of history.

APPENDIX: BATTLE OF LEXINGTON GREEN

	Geocities	Jubilee	Public Bookshelf	WPI	Sons of Revolution	Sylvanus Wood
How many British were present?						
How many Americans were present?						
What did Pitcairn yell?						
Who fired first?						
Did the Americans fire?						
How many Americans died?						
How many Americans were injured?						
How many British died?						
How many British were injured?						

CHAPTER 5

HISTORICAL CAUSALITY

There are so many aspects to teaching history that are vital to creating well-rounded historical thinkers, but one of the most fundamental and most overlooked elements is the idea of causality. Far too many students do not understand the idea of causation, that there are multiple reasons for why historical events occurred and transpired in the way in which they did and that there is not a neat and linear progression from start to finish for a historical event. Creating multiple and frequent opportunities for students to engage in authentic historical inquiry helps students to escape this simple, myopic way of thinking that far too many of our students have become accustomed to utilizing when learning and thinking about historical events.

Many novice historical thinkers approach history as being preordained or as being an easy path that is inevitable. It is easier to see the path looking backwards rather than from the perspective of the agents themselves and looking forward. This is much like the way many would approach finding the correct path of a maze. If one starts from the end, the path towards finding the beginning is quite apparent, but if you start from the beginning, the options are much more numerous (Berkin, 2008). We need to help our students to see the maze of history from the beginning and all of the possibilities available to the agents involved.

In addition, chronological thinking is a major element to enabling students to reason historically (Organization of American Historians, 1995). Without a clear understanding of chronology, when events occurred, and in what order, it is extremely difficult for students compare and contrast events within a time period or to those of the present day and to be able to have the capacity to explain probable causes. Chronology and causation are integral and intertwined elements in enabling students to organize their historical thinking and construct plausible historical narratives.

Recently, I was in a fifth grade classroom and listened as the teacher asked the students as to what caused the beginning of the Second World War. Several students quickly and proudly proclaimed that it was the bombing of Pearl Harbor. The teacher praised the children and moved on the next portion of content to be covered, without batting an eyelash. This troubled me and brought to mind an experience Sam Wineburg had in a high school classroom when students neatly reduced 400 years of racial history in the United States to a one word answer "Predjudice" (Wineburg, 2001). We should not and cannot allow students to neatly package such complex issues and causes into one word answers. Nor should we, as educators, teach them that there is a singular, "correct" answer that can be found when discussing the cause of an historical event (Gillette, 2006; Martin & Wineburg, 2008).

This does not happen just at the elementary school level. In a recent in-service training for secondary history teachers, the facilitator asked the participants what the cause was for the relocation of the Indians during the Trail of Tears. Several answers were provided, including ideas such as the need for the land, racial policies, and greed, but these were not correct, in the eyes of the facilitator. These answers prompted the question "Why were they not removed in 1810, 1805, 1776, or 1620?" Without any answers, a further question was posed, "What was the most important or abundant export from Georgia and Florida at this time?" By the look on their face, several of the participants knew this and chorally stated "citrus." They were sternly informed that they were wrong. A last brave respondent incorrectly attempted "cattle." After several more grueling minutes, the facilitator informed everyone, as if they should have known already that the single cause, of the relocation of the Indians during the time known as the Trail of Tears, was due to the need for access to the white tail deer. They had become extinct in other parts of the Southeastern United States, and thus, it became necessary to move the Indians to other parts to gain access to the white tail deer and their much needed skins.

It is vital that we move away from this way of thinking and allow students to have opportunities to see that historical events have multiple causes and perspectives. They also need to have opportunities to discuss probable causes without having their passion and interest for history immediately stifled. One effective way to go about doing this is to create and share a story, detached from any actual historical content or emotional attachments, for students to analyze for causation and content so that they can come to the realization that multiple causes can and do exist.

When exposing students, of any age, to the idea of causation, one of the most effective methods I have utilized is the story of Cam the Camel (Chapman, 2003; Woodcock, 2005). This is a fictional tale about a camel and his demise due to massive back collapse:

> Once upon a time, there was a camel who went by the name of Cam. After numerous complications during birth, Cam the camel had been born with severe back problems that would affect him throughout his life. Once Cam completed his camel schooling, he decided to join the traveling circus. Unfortunately for Cam, the camel trainer who worked for the circus, Mack the Camel Slayer, was one of the most vicious and vengeful individuals you could ever have the misfortune of meeting. When Mack was a young child, he was involved in a nasty incident that included a camel's foot and his rear end. He hated camels from that moment on and did not trust the "nasty beasts," as he would like to call them.
>
> After several years in the traveling circus, Cam became the star of the Animal Review Show that took place every night under the big top and became the favorite of all the children. Mack thought that a great way to make a little extra money would be to start selling Cam the camel rides for fifty cents per ride. Unfortunately for Cam, Mack did not place any restrictions on the combined weight of the riders and, thus, often allowed multiple riders to sit on Cam's back at the same time. He also forced Cam to give rides all day long, without breaks, until the time of the Animal Review Show each evening. After many months of this, Cam's back problems began to affect his work. Mack thought that Cam's work performance was slipping, so he felt the need to discipline Cam by forcing him to sleep outside in the cold without a proper bed.
>
> Cam continued to perform at a high level, but nothing he ever did was good enough for Mack. One day, Mack thought that it would be great to see how many people he could load onto Cam's back. He thought that he could become famous if he were the one responsible for organizing this feat and even began imagining his name in the Guinness Book of World Records and thought about all of the talk shows on which he would appear. Mack picked up a piece of straw off of the ground and started chewing on it as he brashly began to invite people to be a part of history in the making. He was able to load three adults and four children on Cam's back. Meanwhile, Cam struggled to remain standing and groaned, as the weight of his load became overwhelming. Mack stood back and was proud of his efforts to set a new world record. He then took the piece of straw out of his mouth and casually tossed it onto Cam's back. Cam dropped to his knees, keeled over, and died of massive back collapse.
>
> The main question that arises from all of this is "Was it the straw that broke the camel's back"?

After the story is shared with them, they are broken up into groups of four or five and are asked to highlight all of the causes from story. To take this one step further, they are asked to determine which are necessary causes (N) and which are contributory causes (C). I define necessary causes for them as being any causes that are essential or that the presence of x necessarily implies the presence of y. Contributory causes are defined as causes that help to produce an effect but cannot produce the end results by itself. Once sufficient time to complete this has elapsed, we discuss their thoughts as a class and determine, from their perspective, if it truly was the straw that broke the camel's back. During these discussions, it is found that each group, as well as individual, has different thoughts as to what were necessary causes and contributory causes. We generally agree that it not the straw, in isolation, that broke the camel's back.

The groups are then asked to create their own graphic representation of the demise of Cam the Camel, keeping in mind all of the necessary and contributory causes that they listed. Among the types of graphical representations and organizers utilized by the students are hierarchical graphic organizers, sequential graphic organizers, Venn Diagrams, fact webs, event chains, and pictographs (Gallavan & Kottler, 2007). By leaving the options open, it allows the educator to further examine the choices made by the students and delve deeper into the modes of thinking going on within individual groups.

The last step of this activity is for the students to construct a narrative documenting the life and causes for the death of Cam the Camel. This step is important, as students must have multiple opportunities to construct historical narratives to gain a better understanding of historical causality and how the narratives that they consume have been constructed (Organization of American Historians, 1995). Within the narrative, the students must explicate the problem, the multiple causes (necessary and contributory), the ultimate result, and a detailed discussion of how the elimination of one of the necessary causes would alter the eventual outcome, the passing of Cam the Camel (Lebow, 2007). To assist them in this endeavor, the students are provided with a listing of vocabulary words (i.e., consequently, deterred, exacerbated, initially, subsequently, ultimately, etc.) that can be utilized in the construction of their historical narrative. This helps them to think more deeply about the causes, effects, and ultimate outcome in regards to the life of Cam and enables them to get away from creating a list of items one after another using nondescriptive words such as "next" and "then."

During the discussion and debriefing of this activity as a class, the students are asked what evidence or primary sources would be available for the historian or biographer documenting the life and times of Cam the Camel. After this discussion, they are asked which, if any other, perspectives would be helpful in understanding this individual's life and could be utilized in the construction of a historical narrative or biography based on the life of Cam. Typically, students come up with Mack the Camel Slayer, Cam's family members, and other camels working for Mack and decide that looking at this from multiple perspectives is essential for gaining the best understanding of what may have occurred.

As an optional addition to this, students can be presented initially with just the introduction and conclusion of the story of Cam the Camel. The students can then discuss and debate what is needed to determine what caused Cam's demise, speculate on what events and causes may have been present, and what sources would be helpful for determining this. Then, the students can be exposed to the entire story and conduct the steps outlined above.

Far too often, students, in history classes and textbooks, are presented with a singular cause as to how historical events unfolded (Hicks, 2007). One of the most dangerous practices, by history teachers, is allowing students to believe that there are simple, monocausal explanations for why and how history happens. It is essential that students are exposed to multiple perspectives, representations, and causes as they have the opportunity to investigate history in authentic ways (Levstik & Barton, 2005). It is up to the teacher to allow students to escape historical myopia.

CHAPTER 6

BUILDING HISTORICAL AGENCY

The National Council for the Social Studies (NCSS) defines social studies as "the integrated study of the social sciences and humanities to promote civic competence ... in essence, social studies promotes knowledge of and involvement in civic affairs," and within the mission statement for the NCSS, it is stated that "social studies educators teach students the content knowledge, intellectual skills, and civic values necessary for fulfilling the duties of citizenship in a participatory democracy" (NCSS, 2010, para. 3). These thoughts are echoed in a report released by the Task Force on Character Education in the Social Studies in which they state that "students should both understand the nature of democratic principles and values and demonstrate a commitment to those values and principles in the daily routines of their private and public lives" (NCSS, 1997, para. 7). The Task Force on Standards for Teaching and Learning in the Social Studies notes that "exemplary social studies programs develop social and civic participation skills" (NCSS, 1997).

These are lofty yet worthy goals. Unfortunately, research indicates that children do not see themselves as possessing the power to be change agents and truly having any involvement within civic affairs (den Heyer, 2003b). Generally, children attribute agency, having the power or authority to act, to traditionally celebrated historical figures. Often, this leads to increased apathy about their own future due to the sense that social change is the prerogative of only the most "powerful" of individuals. Agency is an essential part to being a productive citizen in a participatory democracy, and if children are expected to act, they must believe they possess the power to affect change. Shanken (2000) avers, "citizens, in the republican sense, must possess agency and must care about the results of their actions if they are to fulfill their responsibility to construct, maintain, and improve society" (p. 64). Teachers must find ways to instill a sense of agency within their students, in spite of traditional thought. It is essential for history educators to realize that preparing their students to take on the role of citizenship will be an ongoing and crucial process.

Through interactive technologies, such as the Internet, generally available in the average classroom, educators have the potential to revitalize the traditional notions of citizenship education (Mason et al., 2000). Educators need to utilize various technologies, including the Internet, to encourage their student population to engage in disciplined inquiry, perspective taking, and meaning making and assist in the process of "civic learning, deliberation, and action" (Cogan, Grossman, & Liu, 2000, p. 50). Mason et al. (2000) feel that providing examples in the classroom of what is possible when utilizing emerging technologies is a vital first step in preparing teachers to fulfill the mission of history and the social studies. This chapter looks at the notion of agency and ways in which history educators can prepare their student population to become and think of themselves as historical agents through the utilization of the Internet.

Defining the concept of agency has increasingly become a source of strain and confusion (Bandura, 2001; Emirbayer & Mische, 1998). Emirbayer and Mische (1998) note that "variants of action theory, normative theory, and political-institutional analysis have defended, attacked, buried, and resuscitated the concept in often contradictory and overlapping ways" (p. 962). Simply, agency can be thought of as the attainment of a goal through human action or the power people have to exercise control over events that affect their lives (Bandura, 1989, 1999; Levstik & Barton, 2005; Marat, 2003; Sewell, 1992). Emirbayer and Mische (1998) define agency with more complexity by stating that it is:

> the temporally constructed engagement by actors of different structural environments—the temporal-relational contexts of action—which, through the interplay of habit, imagination, and judgment, both reproduces and transforms those structures in interactive response to the problems posed by changing historical situations. (p. 970)

It is felt by some that in order for agency to be present there is a requirement that the actions made by an individual be effective in changing material or cultural conditions and actors involved should possess the ability to examine the consequences of an action and be reflexive in evaluating them (Dietz & Burns, 1992).

It also requires that an individual intentionally make things happen by his or her own course of action while rationally and consciously selecting a means to achieve an end (Bandura, 2001; Dietz & Burns, 1992; Pomper, 1996). This enables individuals to play a role in their own self-development, adaptation, and self-renewal with the situations and environments in which they live (Bandura, 2001).

All human beings involved in a particular situation possess the ability to be an agent, but it is an individual's belief in their own self-efficacy which forms the foundation for human agency (Bandura, 1989, 2001; Dunn, 2000; Sewell, 1992). The capacity for agency is inherent in all human beings, as individuals are born with a capacity for agency, equivalent to one's ability to use language (Sewell, 1992). Higher and more developed levels of agentic competence are determined by:

> a specific range of cultural schemas and resources available in a person's particular social milieu. The specific forms that agency will take consequently vary enormously and are culturally and historically determined. But a capacity for agency is as much a given for humans as the capacity for respiration. (Sewell, 1992, p. 20)

It is essential that an individual not only be aware of his or her capacity for agency but that one believes he or she has the ability to produce desired results as well as forestalling detrimental ones by the course of his or her actions. Regardless of other factors that may operate as guides and motivators, an individual should be rooted in the core belief that he or she has the power to produce effects through action.

Although one may possess self-efficacy, specific social situations and locales affect agentic opportunities as it is possible for an individual to be an agent when facing in one direction but lose that power as soon as he or she is facing in another (Bandura, 1989; Pomper, 1996; Sewell, 1992). Even though much of what people do is to exercise a control over their self-development and life circumstances, there is also a degree of fortuity in the courses lives take. Some of the most significant determinants of life paths transpire through the most trivial of circumstances (Bandura, 2001). Fortuity does not mean that an individual has no control over various effects and courses; agents find ways in which they may capitalize on the fortuitous nature of life.

Human agency is a temporally embedded process that is educated by the past while being oriented both toward the future and the present (Emirbayer & Mische, 1998). The way people come to understand their own relationship to the past, future, and present makes a difference in the actions they take. An individual's changing conception of agentic possibilities greatly influences how they act within different periods and places and how they see these worlds as more or less responsive to human effort and purpose. Agents live simultaneously in the past, future, and present as they engage situations and repertoires from the past, envision hypothetical pathways, and adjust actions in accordance to emerging situations. Agency is always agency towards something, by the methods and means by which individuals enter into relationships with their surrounding environment, people, meanings, and events.

FOUR CORE FEATURES TO HUMAN AGENCY

According to Bandura (2001), there are four core features that are essential elements to human agency: intentionality, forethought, self-reactiveness, and self-reflectiveness. Intentionality refers to the power individuals possess to originate actions for specific purposes and with deliberation. Through forethought, individuals motivate themselves and direct actions in anticipation of events that will occur in the future (Bandura, 1998). One's ability to bring expected outcomes to bear on current situations promotes foresightful behavior (Bandura, 2001). An agent must also possess self-reactiveness, as they must be a planner and a forethinker, but they must also be a self-motivator and regulator. Agency must involve not only an individual's ability to make deliberative choices and plans for action, but the ability to shape appropriate courses of action and to motivate and regulate their implementation. This multifaceted self-directedness functions through a self-regulatory process that links thought to action. The fourth distinctly core human feature of agency is self-reflectiveness, which means that individuals are not only agents of action but also are conscious self-examiners of their own functioning. Agents have the metacognitive capacity to reflect upon themselves and the adequacy of their thoughts and actions.

DIFFERENT MODES OF HUMAN AGENCY: PERSONAL, PROXY, AND COLLECTIVE

There are three different modes of human agency: personal, proxy, and collective (Bandura, 1998, 2001, 2002). Personal agency is that which is exercised individually. Proxy agency is when people secure desired outcomes through influencing others to act on their behalf; and collective agency is when people act simultaneously to shape their shared future.

Personal agency is exercised on an individual basis, as they bear their influence directly upon themselves and their environment. In circumstances when individuals do not have direct control over social conditions and institutional practices around them or lack the willingness to shoulder responsibility over situations for which they command influence, they seek change through proxy agency (Bandura, 2001, 2002). This socially-mediated mode of agency allows individuals to gain desired outcomes through other's access to resources, expertise, influence, or power. Individuals also utilize proxy agency to control situations over which they have the ability to exert direct influence when they believe others can manage the situation better or they do not want to burden themselves with the aspects necessitated by direct control. This form of control has its downside as part of the consequence of proxy agency is the reliance upon the competence, power, and favor of others. In this case, individuals may end up surrendering control to another individual who may not have their best interests in mind (Allen, 1997).

Since individuals do not live within a vacuum, many goals that are sought are only achievable through collective, socially-interdependent efforts by pooling knowledge, skills, and resources, as well as through providing mutual support, forming alliances, and working together so that things that may not be accomplished individually may be secured (Bandura, 2001, 2002). It is the conviction of collective power to generate specific results, rather than simply the sum of their beliefs, that is essential to collective agency. Collective agency is the effort of people acting synchronously on a shared belief, not individual thoughts and efforts of a disembodied group. In order for individuals to function successfully, there is a requirement of a blend of all three modes of agency regardless of cultures within which they reside.

TEACHING/HISTORICAL AGENCY

Agency in history is something that must be addressed in classrooms, as students must come see that they are agents not only in their learning process but also in the greater scope of their lives (Levstik & Barton, 2005). Teachers must address the concept of historical agency as students need to be ready to act when situations arise utilizing what they have learned; unfortunately, history is often told as a story and leaves students unprepared to go beyond this and see agentic opportunities. It is vital that students see and believe that all individuals are participants within the ongoing drama of history as both its subjects and agents. Levstik and Barton (2005) state:

> We make history by the collective activities of our lives, including our participation in both the enduring and ephemeral dilemmas of our times. Unfor-

tunately, history instruction often loses exactly that sense of agency. To the extent that we make history seem both finished and inevitable, students have difficulty seeing themselves as having agency—the power to make history. (p. 125)

Research has suggested students infer that the agency involved in their own communities' social and political formation might best be described as "heroic individuals engaged in individual power struggles" (den Heyer, 2003b, p. 39). Unfortunately, it has been found that students have been taught those individuals in political power are those who hold the ability to be an agent of history. They are being taught and led to believe in a cultural, class, and gender specific ideal of agency that is grossly insufficient. Educators only scratch the surface of the social influence students hold when only briefly discussing social empowerment or attributing historical agency to only those in power positions. We must address the inadequacies of teaching in this manner especially in light of the challenges that will be faced by students in the future; if teachers continue to teach a hyperindividualized heroic notion of agency, students will become apathetic and despondent.

INTERNET/AGENCY

Advancements in electronic technologies have revolutionized the nature, reach, and loci of human influence. Due to the global and decentralized nature of the Internet, small causes can have large effects thus enabling actors to have agency at a distance or from anywhere in the world (Fuchs, 2003). The Internet provides various social forces with alternative modes of action and innovative ways in which they may organize and disseminate agentic action (Wang, 2001).

The accessibility of information disseminated through various media outlets has served to encourage interest in international affairs and provided a way in which an increasing number of citizens can have their voice heard and gain a role in the process of social change (Berson, Berson, & Iannone, 2000/2001). In the past, a student's education was primarily dependent upon the schools to which he or she was assigned, but today the Internet offers immeasurable opportunities for students to guide their own learning and to become actively involved in civic life. They now have immediate access at their fingertips to digital libraries, museums, laboratories, and experts, unobstructed by time or location.

As information becomes more accessible online, it is crucial teachers give ample opportunities for students to develop analytical capabilities and acquire the knowledge and skills to move from apathy to action when addressing social issues. Through computer technologies and materials available online, students gain access to diverse people and perspectives that allow them an opportunity to become actively involved in an increasingly global and interactive world. The following four sections will provide ways in which teachers can promote the three types of agency (personal, proxy, and collective) within their student population through the utilization of various Internet resources as well as a section presenting student-created examples of agency and a site for an instructional guide provided to assist educators in the creation of civic participation projects.

Personal Agency and the Internet

International Schools CyberFair (http://www.globalschoolnet.org/gsncf/index.cfm) is a program used by schools and youth organizations around the world that showcases research conducted by school aged children. CyberFair recognizes and gives awards to the best projects in eight different categories: local leaders, businesses, community organizations, historical landmarks, environment, music, art, and local specialties. This program encourages youth to use technology to share what they have learned and to become advocates for causes that affect their community. The Environmental Awareness and Issues category asks students to design a website that exposes local environmental concerns or that highlights special efforts to promote a sense of awareness and action (i.e., disaster preparedness, floods, earthquakes, hurricanes, beach erosion, solid waste management, water, air, and noise pollution). International Schools CyberFair hopes that through this program students will gain a better understanding of the world around them and take "individual action" for positive change.

Scorecard (http://www.scorecard.org) offers information about pollution problems and toxic chemicals that may be found in the visitor to this site's community and opportunities to learn who is responsible. This site offers further information about companies that are chronic offenders, pollution in different geographic areas, and which racial, ethnic, and income groups historically have endured environmental burdens. Scorecard allows users to take action as informed citizens, by providing them with background knowledge and an opportunity to contact polluting companies, elected representatives, and ways to become more involved in their own community.

Proxy Agency and the Internet

Congress.org (http://www.congress.org) is a private, nonpartisan company that specializes in facilitating civic participation. Through this site, users are able to identify and contact elected leaders in Congress, the

White House, and state legislatures. Congress.org assists users by allowing them to post letters online, read what other Americans are saying to elected officials, and create and post action alerts in order to enlist others interested in a particular issue. Through the site, one also can have their letters printed and hand delivered to Congress. Congress.org helps users find and contact their local and national media outlets and sends out weekly emails with their representative's votes.

SpeakOut.com (http://speakout.com) was started by an individual, Ron Howard, because he was looking for a way in which he could voice his opinion and was not quite sure how to go about accomplishing this. He felt a disconnect with the government and political leaders, so he created this site as a vehicle for connecting people with their elected officials. SpeakOut.com allows its users to learn about various issues and gives an opportunity for them to react. SpeakOut.com is an online opinion research company that allows its users to freely voice their opinion. This site takes the traditional market research focus groups and political polls and puts them online and allows its users to tell politicians, political parties, corporations, marketers and special interest groups how they feel and why. The site also provides interactive polls, ways to send messages to elected officials, and opportunities to sign petitions posted there by others trying to make a difference.

Thomas: Legislative Information on the Internet (http://thomas.loc.gov) was brought online by a team at the Library of Congress brought the Thomas system online in January 1995, acting under the directive of the leadership of the 104th Congress to make Federal legislative information available to the Internet public. In addition to the databases of information available here, the home page provides links of interest and information about how laws are made and the process for the enactment of a law. Within this site, the user can find directories for both the House of Representatives and the Senate. The House site gives users access to an alphabetical list of representatives, with their room assignments and phone numbers, lists by state delegation, and a list of committee assignments. Within the area for the Senate, each senator's name is linked to his or her home page with directory information (room, phone, fax number) as well as other information provided by that senator's office. Thomas also provides links to the websites for other legislative agencies: the House of Representatives, the Senate, the Library of Congress, the Government Printing Office, the General Accounting Office, the Congressional Budget Office, the Architect of the Capitol, and the Office of Technology Assessment.

Vote.com (http://www.vote.com) was designed to give users a voice on important public issues and other topics. This site gives users a chance to speak out and to be heard through a series of topics open for discussion.

When a user votes on a topic listed on the site, Vote.com will send an email to significant decision makers, congressional representatives, senators, and the president, informing them of votes made on Vote.com. Users can also suggest specific topics for discussion to be posted on the site.

Collective Agency and the Internet

Action!Network (http://actionnetwork.org) is a site that links users to online activism centers for over 170 leading environment, health and population advocacy organizations. Action Network partners mobilize users through the use of email, by allowing them to consider issues and by sending personalized email messages to key local, national, and world policymakers. Visitors to the site are given an opportunity to browse and join active campaigns that have been posted by other users.

Amnesty International (http://www.amnesty.org) is an independent organization that defines itself as "a worldwide movement of people who campaign for internationally recognized human rights." Their goal is to see a world where everyone can enjoy all that is outlined in the Universal Declaration of Human Rights and other international human rights standards. Amnesty International's mission is to engage in research and to take action against abuses of the rights to physical and mental integrity, freedom of conscience and expression, and freedom from discrimination. Amnesty International works to improve human rights around the world through the actions of ordinary people, which has consistently been acknowledged through the voices of victims who have been assisted through the actions of Amnesty International.

ePALS Classroom Exchange (http://www.epals.com) provides school-safe email and collaborative technologies that are utilized in over 191 countries and by more than 4.6 million students and educators in order to employ the Internet for communication and cross-cultural learning. ePALS began as a place where teachers, interested in utilizing technology to assist collaborative learning, could connect their students with students in other areas around the globe. Not only does this site provide tools and a meeting place for students throughout the world, it offers ideas for ways to enact change through collaboration and areas where students may contribute their views on various matters. During its existence, the United Nations, the U.S. Department Health and Human Services, the White House, and the Canadian Prime Minister's Office all have been groups that have worked with ePALS on collaborative projects with K-16 schools.

Free the Children (http://freethechildren.org) is an international network of children helping children at local, national, and international levels through representation, leadership, and action. The site was founded by Craig Kielburger in 1995, when he was 12 years old. The principal goal of Free the Children is to not only free children throughout the world from poverty and exploitation but to allow young people to see that they are not powerless to bring about positive social change and that they can improve the lives of their peers. The site notes Free the Children is not like other children's charity organizations, as it is an organization "by, of, and for children" that embraces the notion that young people can be leaders in the pursuit of creating a more just, equitable, and sustainable world. Free the Children has been actively involved in bringing the issue of child exploitation squarely on the agenda of the international community and in helping children to find solutions to issues of interest to them and their peers. Free the Children's accomplishments have been recognized by many organizations around the world, including the United Nations.

Voices of Youth (http://www.unicef.org/voy/index.php) began in 1995 as a way in which young people could send messages to the world leaders at the World Summit for Social Development, held in Copenhagen in 1995 and as part of the celebration for UNICEF's 50th Anniversary. From its inception, Voices of Youth was created in hopes of making sure that young people from throughout the world could learn more, say more, and do more about the world in which they live. Through comments from children from more than 100 countries, the Voices of Youth website has been broken down into three distinct areas where its visitors can explore, speak out, and take action. By joining Voices of Youth, the visitor can join in discussions with children around the world and "speak out." UNICEF insures that children's comments are heard throughout the globe by including them within Voices of Youth's bimonthly newsletter, *What Young People Are Saying*, in many UNICEF publications, including the flagship annual report *The State of the World's Children*, and through representatives at United Nations conferences and events. The Voices of Youth site notes that "everybody—and every generation—has a chance to change the world. Your chance is now if you want it." Through their site, the Voices of Youth program shows children how together they can make a difference in the world.

The *Youth Leadership Initiative* (http://www.youthleadership.net) is a nonprofit, nonpartisan national civic education program that was created in order to involve children in the American electoral and policymaking process. In efforts to achieve their objectives, the Youth Leadership Initiative offers technology-based resources that promote long-term civic engagement, as well as producing technology-based projects that bring the American democratic process to the classroom. This program is dedicated to the idea that "government works better when politics work better, and that politics works better when citizens are informed and active participants." They believe this process begins with our nation's youngest citizens.

EXAMPLE AND INSTRUCTIONAL GUIDE

StopFamilyViolence.org (http://www.stopfamilyviolence.org) is the result of one woman's awareness of how the Congress' failure to reauthorize the Violence Against Women Act (VAWA) was going to impact her community. Her determination at the grassroots level helped secure the passage of VAWA through the creation of StopFamilyViolence.org. Her site allowed visitors the opportunity to identify their legislators and contact them and the media directly about this crisis; her efforts contributed over 164,000 messages to Congress in support of VAWA. President Clinton signed legislation, which included VAWA, into law on October 28, 2000, so in 12-weeks time, Irene Weiser helped move a stagnant issue into one that saw a 100% increase in funding for the Violence Against Women Act.

The *Constitutional Rights Foundation: Implementing a Civic Action Project* (http://www.crf-usa.org) offers teachers a short guide which details a nine-step process for empowering their students through the planning and implementation of civic participation projects based in their own community. Teachers can download materials (The Six Basic Steps of an Action Project, Project Plan, Project Ideas, and Organizations Concerned with Violence) for use in the classroom. The Six Basic Steps of an Action Project gives students an overview of six steps they can take to complete an action project: (1) select a problem to work on; (2) research the problem; (3) choose a project; (4) plan the project; (5) do the project; and, (6) evaluate what you have done. A project plan is provided to help students with the process of planning an action project. It gives users a step-by-step guide for planning a project and filling out a project plan. The project ideas area lists ideas for projects in which children might choose to address issues of violence, terrorism, and healing. The section, entitled Organizations Concerned with Violence, provides the user with places to look for information and support around issues of violence in their community.

CONCLUSION

When young people are informed of agentic opportunities and are armed with the most current information and multiple perspectives, their awareness can increase motivation to initiate civic action on behalf of those in need. By educating our youth, we can empower these children to become change agents in the future and overcome apathetic and disparaging mentalities and replace them with desires for action. Through the power of the Internet, every individual has the ability to serve as an agentic force for change within our society. The Internet provides a way for individuals to fulfill promises of democracy and to become empowered agents for social change. It has the capacity of providing users with effective tools to supply them with opportunities for exercising their freedom of speech, protecting their rights, and facilitating action. Educators need to embrace the opportunities presented by the Internet and other technologies in order to prepare their student population to become participating citizens in an increasingly global community.

CHAPTER 7

UTILIZING METHODS OF INTEREST TO DIGITAL NATIVES

It is undeniable that students today are fundamentally different than those of previous generations. A large reason for why students of this generation do not enjoy history (Allen, 1994; Black & Blake, 2001; Jensen, 2001; Zhao & Hoge, 2005) is the fact that the curriculum, with which they are presented, is outdated and of little interest to the majority of our student population; it was not designed for students in the digital age and does not attend to the ways in which they learn. The majority of the curriculum, in use, was created by digital immigrants, those individuals who were born prior to the digital revolution and typically do not think, as our students do, in a digital first mentality (Prensky, 2001). Students today are what are known as "digital natives," those individuals who were born in this digital age and know only a world in which they are continuously surrounded by digital technologies, applications, and resources. Thus, it is vital, to the preservation of history as a K-16 content area, that history educators reinvigorate the history curriculum and teach in a manner that is geared toward these digital natives. Prensky (2001) posits that it is "just dumb (and lazy) of educators—not to mention ineffective—to presume that (despite their traditions) the digital immigrant way is the only way to teach, and that the digital natives' 'language' is not as capable as their own of encompassing any and every idea" (p.6). One way to do that is to integrate history teaching with available digital resources and to allow students opportunities to conduct authentic digital history based inquiries.

History is better suited for the digital age and for the utilization of available technologies than any other humanistic discipline (Ayers, 1999). History educators should take advantage of the resources accessible to them as they assist students in the process of constructing historical narratives. We do know that there are multiple resources for acquiring primary and secondary sources, but evidence suggests that their use within the history classroom has been limited (Lee, 2002; Hicks, Doolittle, & Lee, 2004). As many of the historical archives made available on the Internet do not provide interpretations, this allows the perfect avenue for realizing the complexity and highly problematic nature of history (Lee, 2002). Students can have authentic ventures into the past through historical inquiry based investigations (Levstik & Barton, 2005) in ways never imagined in the past. Educators need to think past the traditional ways in which history has been documented; if we allow our students intellectual and technological flexibility, the available "digital archives might move us toward more complex, more literary, forms of narrative" (Ayers, 1999). This approach to learning about the past and constructing historical narratives utilizing digital resources, known as digital history, has been defined as "the study of the past using a variety of electronically reproduced primary source texts, images, and artifacts as well as the constructed historical narratives, accounts, or presentations that result from digital historical inquiry"(Lee, 2002, para 5).

Lee (2002) points out that despite obvious similarities, digital historical resources are distinctly different from nondigital materials:

1. digital historical resources are more accessible;
2. they encourage increased archival activity;
3. they promote the development of social networks;
4. they are easier to manipulate;
5. they are searchable;
6. they are more flexible; and
7. they include an organizational strategy related to the content of the collection (para. 12).

There are myriad ways in which history can and has been taught, but several general best practices for history instruction should be followed, especially when encountering a digital native population.

UTILIZING SOURCES OTHER THAN TRADITIONAL WEBSITES: ONLINE AUCTIONS

As history education continues to be marginalized more and more with each passing day, educators find themselves looking for new ways to creatively and effectively bolster historical content knowledge in their students with less and less financial support. One such resource that can be a history educator's best friend, and one that may not immediately come to mind, are online auction sites (e.g., eBay, uBid, WeBidz, Yahoo Auctions). For those not familiar with online auctions, they are utilized in much the same way as face-to-face auctions, for selling items ranging from antiques to sports collectables to electronics to cars and homes, only they are now able to reach a broader audience. Many educators might not think of online auctions as resources that could be utilized, but many of the items for sale there can be found to directly pertain to the content covered in most history courses. The items available for sale open opportunities for utilizing primary sources and exposing students to multiple perspectives, as well as allowing them to see cultural artifacts from all over the world and various items they otherwise might never have the opportunity to see.

Similar to the marketing of a home, sellers create an advertisement of the item for sale, which includes: a title, description, and pictures for the item for sale; location of the seller; and beginning sale price and shipping and handling charges. As with items being auctioned in a traditional format, a beginning bid price is set, as well as a time table for the duration of the auction. Users are able to submit a single bid, a maximum bid, or may have an opportunity to buy the item at a desired price preset by the seller.

As a history educator, these artifacts for sale may be utilized in a variety of ways. These artifacts can be included in an artifact bag set (also known as Jack Dawes sets), used for an artifact naming and inquiry assignment, can be scanned for use in student created documentary films, or as a prompt for a creative writing assignment; all of which may be used as an introductory activity, elements of a unit, or even as an assessment tool.

One important thing that users should be aware of prior to purchasing anything through an online auction site is the seller's ratings and shipping and handling charges. Buyers are encouraged to provide details of their buying experience, so as a potential buyer, you should review some of the previous transactions of the seller and look at the seller's rating and number of positive and negative reviews provided. I have found that many of the sellers with high ratings and numerous items for sale turn out to be antique dealers who have found a new medium for selling their wares. Thus, many of the sellers are quite knowledgeable about the items that they sell and have done some research prior to purchasing the item themselves. As with any purchase made, the buyer must beware and should carefully read the transaction stipulations, in order to protect themselves and be sure that the item for sale is what is expected. Sellers typically welcome questions from the potential buyer, so you should feel free to contact them to clarify any questions had about the item for sale prior to purchase. Out of over three hundred transactions purchasing historical memorabilia on online auction sites, I have only had one negative experience, with the item that was purchased ($5.00) never being received.

Budgets for purchasing of history-based instructional materials is often minimal or nonexistent, so educators may want to use online auctions as electronic resources for bolstering their own knowledge about a topic of study or for printing off the images of the items for sale there, as they are typically quite clear and of a high level of quality. The descriptions can help create background or supplemental information for history teachers and, depending on their age, for students, as well. As the images provided are typically of a high quality, educators can select the image posted for an item for sale and save them for printing and for use in a variety of ways.

One area, within most online auction sites, that I have found to be most useful is the "collectables" section. Within the collectables section, items for sale here are typically categorized within subgroups, such as historical memorabilia, photographic images, advertising, cultures, ethnicities, and militaria ranging in time periods dating from pre-1700 to the present day.

One specific example, from the collectables section, that I have found to be valuable in my teaching is the area related to the home front in the United States during the Second World War. For example, when searching eBay (www.ebay.com) for items related to the American home front during the Second World War, I follow the links provided in the directory from militaria to WWII to United States to homefront. This section typically has anywhere from 600 to 1,000 items for sale at any one point in time. As this is a continually updated auction site, various items can be found there and are different each time a visitor comes to the site. Included among the hundreds of items that I have purchased from online auctions pertaining to the American home front are: ration stamp books, magazines, letters, diaries, photo albums, advertisements, posters, and war bonds booklets. Once again, I could have chosen to save or print off the images for sale rather than purchasing them, if funds were not available for this purpose.

I have used these primary source artifacts in a variety of ways, but one of my favorite uses is in the creation of artifact bag sets to introduce students to life in the United States during the Second World War. In groups of four or five, the students view the artifacts in the set one by one and

Figure 7.1. Contents of an artifact bag.

determine the significance of each and how each relates to life in the United States during this time period. They are also asked to group items in their bag into related themes or topics. Once sufficient time to view all of the items in the artifact bag has elapsed, I ask for a volunteer to share an item of interest with the entire class. I allow them to discuss its relevance to the overall theme and what made this particularly interesting to the group. I am able to then ask the class for any other items relating to this theme, which brings all of the other groups into the conversation. I allow the students to dictate the flow of the lesson and only talk when clarification is needed. At the conclusion of the lesson, the students have a better understanding of what life was like in the United States during the Second World War and that rationing, recycling, and conservation were important concepts to life during this time period. Due to the nature of the artifacts being used, clear images and artifacts with minimal text, this process allows students of all ability, grade, English proficiency levels to be included in the discussion and the learning process. This lesson can be concluded by allowing each student to choose one of the items from their bag, or one preselected by the teacher, as a writing prompt; they are encouraged to keep the following journalistic questions in mind when responding to the importance of the item: who, what, where, when, why, and how.

The Annenberg Media website has a section on "Social Studies in Action: Using Primary Sources" (http://www.learner.org/channel/libraries/socialstudies/3_5/waffle/reflect.html) that provides a plethora of ideas, handouts, and videos to assist classroom teachers when incorporating primary sources into history teaching. Some ideas include:

- Have students analyze a primary source, asking questions such as, Who wrote the source? Why? When? Where? and What were the consequences? Then have students analyze another primary source about the same event that provides a different point of view. Ask students to compare the sources, suggest reasons for the different points of view, discuss the credibility of each source, and reflect on how they might determine which point of view best represents the event.
- Ask students to choose a topic of interest and find primary sources related to that topic. Ask them what each source can teach them about the topic. Discuss whether the authors of the sources have different points of view about the topic and why they might hold those views.
- Introduce several types of graphic organizers to your students over time. Then select several primary sources and ask students to use the graphic organizers to represent the main points of each source.
- After working in pairs or groups to analyze and interpret primary sources, ask students to reflect on how this method is helpful to their learning.

There are numerous sites on the Internet that provide ideas for how to incorporate primary sources into the teaching of history content. One great place to start is the Library of Congress' American Memory website (http://memory.loc.gov). Teachers can find primary source sets, lesson plans, activities, handouts, etc. related to the use of primary source artifacts with students of every grade level. Another site is the Smithsonian Center for Education and Museum Studies web, especially the section dedicated to the use of primary sources (http://www.smithsonianeducation.org/idealabs/ap/guide/index.htm), which has broken down its resources into six sections: Generating Questions about Artifacts; Artifact Study; Document Analysis; Comparing Artifacts and Documents; Artifacts in Historical Context; and Skill Building and Writing. Additional sites providing educators with resources and ideas for utilizing primary sources include: History Now (http://www.historynow.org); The National Archives (http://www.archives.gov/education/lessons); PBS Teachers (http://www.pbs.org/teachers/socialstudies); and ProTeacher! Using primary sources in the social studies curriculum (http://www.proteacher.com/090093.shtml).

In addition to the primary source artifacts available on online auction sites, a great selection of children's literature are offered for purchase there. I have purchased many terrific titles, even in hard bound, for around $5.00 and have found most to be near brand new in quality. Half.com (www.half.com) is one part of the eBay site that specifically sells books, music, etc. at a set price rather than in the auction style format, so that is an option for those skeptical about the auction format of online auction sites but want to utilize all that eBay has to offer.

Online auction sites can be some of the most valuable resources available to the history educator. One can find artifacts related to just about every topic imaginable, and sellers provide detailed information, high quality images, and often a different or more detailed perspective of the items for sale. One key to avoiding frustration with the buying process is remembering that buyers must be ware, as with any purchases electronically or in person. Another suggestion for users is to remember and employ the same list of criteria (like the one provided by Cornell University Library http://www.library.cornell.edu/olinuris/ref/research/webcrit.html) used when evaluating any electronic based resource or Internet sites, as online auction sites are not exempt from the inclusion of incorrect or inaccurate information. For creative educators who like to think outside of the box, just about all of what can be found on online auction sites can be utilized in many ways within the history classroom.

TIMELINES FOR BUILDING HISTORICAL UNDERSTANDING

Timelines can be utilized to help students visualize how historic periods relate to other time frames. Primary sources and images can be added to timelines to help students see changes in social, cultural, and political life throughout historic periods. Students can also bring in photographs and images printed from the Internet to add to these timelines. Digital video editing software can make timelines truly come alive.

The first step in the process of creating an electronic timeline is obviously to decide upon a topic for the timeline. Students then gather digital images from the Internet, taking pictures with digital still cameras, or by scanning in images and other artifacts with a scanner and computer. Once the images are saved on the computer or on a data storage device, students can use digital video editing software to add these images to their project timeline. Since the order of the images can be altered easily by dragging and dropping an image to a new location on the timeline, this also builds students capacity to understand sequencing and chronological order. Students can then insert transitions in the timeline so that the images move to the next visual smoothly and with a more professional look. Transitions are inserted between images or used as a fade-in at the beginning of the timeline or a fade-out at the end. Audio tracks can easily be added to timelines to create an even more enjoyable presentation. Students can add voiceovers to provide an explanation of the images or about the topic covered in the timeline, which allows the history teacher an additional opportunity to assess the students' historical knowledge acquisition. Volume levels for the voiceovers can be adjusted using the software, so both the voiceover and music can effectively be intertwined. Titles, sound effects and closing credits are great enhancements that add interest and spark to the creation of timelines. All of these effects can be added smoothly and effectively. Electronic visual timelines are a great way of presenting gathered information and learning about historical content in a manner that is natural for digital natives.

VIRTUAL HISTORY: INSERTING STUDENTS BACK INTO THE PAST

In a recent conversation with a class of eighth grade history students about life on the American home front during World War II, the students' inability to visualize and contextualize the past was blatantly clear. When asked how they thought Americans on the home front during the Second World War got information about the ongoing war in Europe, many of them responded with CNN Headline News or the Internet. It was beyond many of the students to grasp that American homes were not equipped with Internet connections during World War II and that many homes did not have televisions.

For history teachers, it is a struggle to find ways to help students conceptualize the past and think historically. Virtual history projects such as the one described here can provide a powerful method of helping students engage in historical inquiry. Virtual history projects, as defined for this instructional application, are projects in which a student's photograph is digitally placed within a historical photograph. Using digital images of students and of historical images to transport students back in time increase not only students' excitement level, but it also helps students visualize and personalize the past.

Allowing students to "visit" another time and place can bring a new level of understanding of history for many students. Virtual history projects require that students engage in an inquiry process that supports their understanding of the big ideas in history. When students engage in historical inquiry, they develop the schemas, or mental scaffolds that help clarify the major concepts in the field and identify when to apply those concepts. Developing these schemas helps students move from being a novice in the field to being an expert (Bransford, 2000). This particular virtual history project prompts students to go beyond the stark memorization of facts, and develop a conceptual understanding of the past. In this sense, students are better able to understand and apply historical concepts and begin to move from novice to expert comprehension.

Inquiry is the act of using prior knowledge, asking questions, identifying new information, and developing conclusions. "Placing" students back in time invites them to engage in an inquiry process that allows them to personalize and recreate an event or era in the past. It is essential for teachers to ask questions in virtual history projects that require students to investigate and interpret the digital image. Teachers should prompt students to analyze the photograph by asking students questions such as: What is happening in this photograph? What are you doing in this photograph? What would you like to do next? From where you are in the photograph, describe what you hear. What are people talking about around you? What are you saying to the people around you? How do you feel at this time? What makes you feel this way?

Virtual history projects are grounded in Erikson's (1968) theory of development. That is, many students are in constant search to develop their ego identity. By virtually placing themselves back into time or into other settings, students engage in the unfolding process that contributes to personal development. Adolescents develop based on the links between interrelated environments (Garbarino, 1985). They make sense of themselves through a series of concentric circles. The adolescent is in the center of the circle, while family, peers, school and community fill the immediate surrounding circles. Events in history are often found in circles that are a great distance from the adolescent. By virtually placing students into historical events, through virtual history projects, teachers are able to help students bridge the gap from students' immediate world to distant times and places.

To begin, you must have an historical photograph, a digital image of the student, and a computer with Adobe Photoshop or similar software such as Microsoft Photo Editor. Adobe Photoshop is not the only software package that will allow the user to edit digital images, although it is generally considered one of the best. Many of the free or lower priced image editing software packages will allow the user to crop and rotate images but do not allow for more complex operations as the ones described here. Prior to purchasing a full version of any of the software packages, try the trial versions which are typically available on the manufacturer's website free of charge.

The historical photograph can either come from scanning an photograph you took or by searching the Internet. Many search engines, such as Google (www.google.com) have an option on their search page that will let you choose to only search for images. If you use a photograph from the Internet, make sure that you are using an image that does not have copyright restrictions that forbid its use in this manner. Most Internet sites that provide digital images include a disclaimer or copyright restrictions for the use of items found within their site. Although individuals using images for educational purposes may not need to ask for permission when using them in multimedia presentations and other educational projects, they should be sure to cite the source of the images used unless specifically requested not to do so. Many sites exist that provide public domain images for consumption for educational purposes. A helpful site for locating these resources is entitled Public Domain Pictures (http://www.princetonol.com/groups/iad/links/clipart.html). One site created specifically to provide teachers with images for educational use is Pics4Learning (http://www.pics4learning.com). It is essential to carefully read any copyright notices posted on a website providing digital images for further restrictions and instructions. As a general rule, all works available on the Internet are copyrighted which means that they may have restrictions upon their use. For complete information on copyright regulations, visit the U.S. Copyright Office website (http://www.copyright.gov).

Once an acceptable image is found, it is important to save the image at the highest resolution available in order to have greater clarity and more options for its use. The most common error performed by people searching for graphics on the Internet is that they save the digital file from the "thumbnail" sized image on a website. Many times when the thumbnail image is saved directly, it has a smaller file size and in turn has a poorer quality than a larger option that might be available on the same website. It is essential to click upon the thumbnail image whenever possible to open a larger and higher quality image before saving. Another important key to saving higher quality images is that when given the option for the type of file for which the image will be saved, it is best to save it as a jpeg, a file that has a name that ends in .jpg or .jpeg. Jpegs often will preserve the quality of the image better than other file types (i.e., bitmaps or gifs). You can get the image of the student in several ways, but the three easiest ways are to take a digital picture of him/her with a digital camera or to take a photograph of the student that has already been developed and scan it into the computer by using a scanner.

Once you have digital copies of both the historical artifact and the photograph of the subject to be inserted, you should mentally map out how the final product will look. You must think it through carefully, as it will

Figure 7.2.

make the process much easier once you sit down at the computer to alter the historical artifact.

Begin the alteration process by opening Adobe Photoshop and both of the image files you will be working with on this project. You can do that by clicking on "File" in the top tool bar and selecting "Open." This is similar to the process used in most software packages when opening a file. Once you have both images open, you should begin with sizing both of the images so that they are approximately the same size. Also, be sure that the size of the student image is relative to the artifacts in the historical image. Make sure both windows are being viewed at 100%. To make sure, go to "View" at the top tool bar and choose "Actual Pixels."

To begin the alteration process, make sure the picture that are inserting into the historical artifact is highlighted with the top of the picture box having a blue border. If it is not highlighted, click once on the photograph to be inserted, and the border should turn blue. To change the size of the image click on "Image" on the top tool bar and select "Image Size." In the newly opened box, type in a smaller number in the pixel dimension width area, if the insert needs to be smaller, and a larger number, if it needs to be larger. The height will automatically change with the width if you have the "Constrain Proportions" box check marked. Click on "OK" and the changes take effect. Continue these steps until you find a good size, as there is no steadfast rule that can be used when importing images from different sources, as they will tend to differ in size. If you are ever unhappy with what you just did, choose "Window" on the top tool bar and select "Show History." In the "History" tool bar area, you can go back as many steps as you want.

Once you have the images at appropriate sizes to one another, you are ready to cut out the image of the person and place it within the historical artifact. In the Photoshop side tool bar, click and hold the lasso icon; it is the one that looks like a piece of rope and is located in the second position from the top on the left side. Once you click and hold on this location, you will be presented with several options. Choose the one that appears to be a lasso with a magnet, which will appear as the icon on the far right.

Once you release the mouse button over the magnetic lasso, you will be ready to begin the cutting process. Move the lasso over the edge of the area to be cut, click the left mouse button to begin the cutting. Trace the area to be cut around the shape and return to the starting point. If the area does not become highlighted with dotted lines or the "marching ants," press the "Enter" key or try again. If you make an error, click on the word "Select" on the top tool bar and choose "Deselect." Follow these steps again.

To make fine adjustments, press and hold the "Ctrl" key while also pressing the "+" or the "-" keys on the keyboard to zoom in and out on the photograph. Find an area to be fine-tuned. Select the lasso from the tool bar, which is also the left lasso when clicking and holding on the lasso icon. In the area to be fine-tuned, hold "Shift" for adding area that is missing from the "marching ants" and "Alt" for removing an area included in the dotted lines. Using the mouse and holding the corresponding key, make a loop of the area to be added or removed. When the mouse button is released, the desired changes will go into effect.

Sometimes you will find that the colors or brightness between the two photographs is quite contrasting. If the brightness or color is different in the two photos, go to "Image" in the top tool bar and choose "Adjust" and "Brightness/Contrast" or "Hue/Saturation." Experiment with different levels to find a good match. If you are wanting to remove the color from an image to create a black and white photograph, then click on "Image," "Mode," and "Grayscale" in the top menu bar. Remember that you can always use the "History" option if you make a terrible or unwanted alteration.

Now you are ready to insert the cut selection into the historical artifact. Click on the "Move Tool" icon in the side tool bar. The "Move Tool" is the icon located in the top right corner that looks like an arrow. Once the area to be cut and moved is highlighted with dotted lines, move the tool over the section to be cut and scissors should appear. Click and hold over the section to be moved. Move the mouse to the general area in the original in which it is to be placed. There should be a plus icon over the original, meaning the insert item is to be added there. Release the mouse button and the outlined selection will be inserted into the artifact. Now that the image of the person is in the original, you can use the move tool to place it in the correct spot. If the sizing is not right for the insert you should delete it from the original and follow the steps from sizing the insert through this point. The easiest way to do that is to right click over the inserted item and choose "Layer 1" with a left click. Now, go to Layers in the top tool bar and choose "Delete Layer." Attempting to resize the insert in the original may change the sizing of everything in the original.

If you are attempting to place a person in the background of an historic image behind other people or objects found in that image, then you must perform the same steps with each of the items that should appear to be on top of the inserted person. Make sure that you are working with the original historical image by highlighting in blue that layer in the "Layers" popup window. That layer can be opened by clicking on "Window" and "Show Layers" in the top menu bar. The main layer will often be referred to as the "Background" layer. You can also click on the eye icon in the "Layers" window to toggle between being able to view a layer and making it disappear. This makes it much easier to cut out items on one layer without having to see all the layers at once. Make sure that the layer you intend to work with is highlighted in blue as you may be working on a different layer, although it is not currently visible. Open a new window by clicking on "File" and "New" in the top menu bar so that you have a blank window in which you can drag a copy of the cut (Figure 15). Once the person is located in the proper location, you can bring the copy of the object cut from the historical image and place it in its original location to make the person appear behind it.

You now have a finished product in which you can print out, add to a website, or use in any way you choose. The great thing at this point is that you can save the project so that you can come back and alter it later and place other people in the historical photograph. You can also save it as a digital image file for printing or other uses. To save it as a project, you must go under "File" in the top tool bar and choose "Save As." Save the project under a name of your choice; something that you will remember. This will enable you to come back and work on this same picture at a later date. You can also save this as a digital image so that you can use it in a number of ways more easily. To do this, you should click on "File" and choose "Save a Copy." On the "Save As" line, you can choose from a number of format styles. One of the more common digital image file types is

JPEG, so if you do not have a file type in mind that you want to use, JPEG's are a good selection.

This virtual history project is an example of how technology can be used to enhance teaching and learning in the middle school history classroom. Virtual history projects engage students in the act of historical inquiry and invite students to more deeply explore people, places, and events from distant times and locations. The engagement and increased interest levels of students of all ability levels will be a testament to the importance to meeting the needs of digital natives using creative and appealing approaches.

CONCLUSION

Traditionally, primary sources have rarely been used in history classrooms. This has been due, primarily, to the lack of availability of primary sources and to the lack of time teachers have to locate primary sources. In recent years, however, technology has allowed educators to connect with resources outside of the classroom (Dawson & Harris, 1999; Mason et al., 2000). These digital sources give students greater access to primary source materials and provide resources for educators (International Society for Technology in Education, 2004). It is essential that history teachers scaffold their students' learning process, especially when investigating primary sources on the Internet. Terrific ancillary materials and guiding worksheets can be found from the National Archives and Records Administration (http://www.archives.gov/education/lessons/worksheets), the Library of Congress (http://memory.loc.gov/learn/lessons/media.html), and the Maryland Historical Society (http://www.mdhs.org/teachers/worksheets.html).

These sorts of investigations are vital as history students must have opportunities to ask historical question of personal interest to focus the inquiry, engage in the evaluation of historical primary sources, develop conclusions based upon evidence, and create historical knowledge (Barton & Levstik, 2004). Students must understand that historians analyze historical evidence, make choices, and corroborate sources in the construction of historical narratives (Ayers, 1999; History Matters site). Several sites that can assist history educators in this endeavor are Why Historical Thinking Matters (http://historicalthinkingmatters.org/why.html), All about Explorers (http://www.allaboutexplorers.com) and The Mystery of Sam Smiley (https://filebox.vt.edu/users/tsnedike/ssweb/index.html).

CHAPTER 8

ENGAGING IN AUTHENTIC HISTORICAL INQUIRY BY INVESTIGATING HISTORY CLOSE TO THE LEARNER (LOCAL HISTORY)

History teachers are continually seeking new ways in which they can actively involve their students and allow them to think more creatively. Stevens (2001) stated that "because of the way history is generally written and taught, it lacks the richness of content that creates excitement for the young mind" (p. xi). The need for a focus on educating children how what happened in the past affects the present has not vanished. It is even more vital at the local level. It is human nature to understand that which is close to us.

One of the most beneficial ways of allowing students to connect what they already know is through the focusing upon the lives of people in the past (Wellman & Gelman, 1992). Levstik and Barton (1997) contended that "people are one of the subjects that children understand best; even from a very young age, they can reason about the beliefs and intentions of others" (p. 12). Children learn best when it makes human sense, as they understand situations in terms of how they involve people (Donaldson, 1978). Effective use of history, especially social, local, and oral history, in the history curriculum allows students to engage in meaningful historical inquiry, utilize historical thinking skills, and build on prior knowledge by facilitating examination of historical content through first-hand accounts of lived experiences. This approach to the teaching and learning of history facilitates the transfer of knowledge for students of all ages.

Conducting local or community history projects fosters interest in history as it facilitates historical inquiry, creative thinking, and active student engagement through allowing students an opportunity to assume ownership over their own learning rather than being reliant upon directions from the teacher (Clarke & Lee, 2004; Levstik & Barton, 2005; Penyak & Duray, 1999; Quest, 2006; Woods, 2001). Creating local history projects allows students to look beyond the information on the pages of their text and forces them to look deeper into the history of their local environment. Kinsley (1994) notes:

> In our own century, John Dewey, and more recently, Ralph Tyler and Hilda Taba have reminded us that students who actually do things, who engage in activities related to school subjects, learn more efficiently, more effectively, and remember what they have learned much longer than students who don't. (p. 40)

Community and local history projects do just that—ask students to "actually do things" and engage in authentic activities directly related to the study of history.

Community history projects also meet many of the standards laid out by the National Center for History in the Schools (1996) in their *National Standards for History*, especially in regards to their guidelines for historical thinking. The National Center for History in the Schools (1996) states that it is essential for students to be able to "think chronologically, comprehend a variety of sources, engage in historical analysis and interpretation, conduct historical research, and engage in historical issues-analysis and decision making" (pp. 17-24). It is also asserted within the standards that, by grade four, students should understand the differences between family life now and in the recent past versus life long ago, as well as having an understanding of the history of his or her local community. The National Council for the Social Studies Curriculum Standards emphasizes that students should be able to "identify and use various sources for reconstructing the past, such as documents, letters, diaries, maps, textbooks, photos, and others" (National Council for the Social Studies, 1994, p. 34). The National Council for the Social Studies (2002) also states that "A primary goal of public education is to prepare students to be engaged and effective citizens" (para. 1), which includes "instruction on the people, history, and traditions that have shaped our local communities" (para. 6). Carefully designed community history projects offer an opportunity for students to meet all of these standards by engaging in historical inquiry in authentic and meaningful ways.

Solomon (1997) posits that, in order for teachers to be creative, they must "draw upon the community and its people and use the ideas and experiences of the students themselves as important inputs for learning" (p. 289). Thus, local history projects are a good basis for accomplishing these goals, as they involve the students in their own learning while becoming more knowledgeable about the society in which they live versus those of a previous time period (Black & Blake, 2001). Penyak and Duray (1999) note that "problematic questions help focus group discussions, teach important skills, and foster social interaction" (p. 69). Additionally, well-posed research questions may lead to differing opinions as the research is conducted, helping students access and decipher different points of view related to how history "really happened" (Waring, 2007).

Helmreich (1989) provides a sound rationale for emphasizing the study of local history because it "gives people a sense of participation in history" (p. 313). Not only must students collect data and ask intelligent, thought-provoking questions, they will be given an opportunity to analyze their findings and understand that one of the benefits of studying history is that "it deals with values and gives perspective on human existence" (Helmreich, 1989, p. 310). Avery, Avery, and Williams (1994) contend that, when their students create local history projects, they "practice deductive and inductive reasoning, form generalizations about eras in history, analyze connections between technological advances and historical events, and synthesize what they had learned to form clearer historical perspectives" (p. 272).

Some of the ways and resources that can be used when conducting local histories in the K-16 classrooms will be presented here, although the first sources that should be consulted when creating a history of a community are William P. Filby's *Directory of American Libraries With Genealogy or Local History Collections* and Dina C. Carson's *Directory of Genealogical and Historical Societies, Libraries, and Periodicals in the US and Canada* (2006), which contain lists of libraries and societies in the United States that contain local history collections. As educators, we need to utilize the communities in which we live, because they offer a wealth of opportunities for learning and continue to be one of the least tapped resources for history teaching (Martorella, 1998a).

ORAL HISTORIES

A great way to begin a local history project is to utilize the knowledge of its residents through the use of oral histories (Campbell, 2005; Dillon, 2000; Hickey, 1991; Levstik & Barton, 2005; Penyak & Duray, 1999). The process of creating oral histories involves gathering historical information, usually tape-recorded or videotaped, through interviews with persons having firsthand knowledge and documenting it through written transcribed accounts. Students can truly gain a better understanding for the content by interviewing people from the community, which can really bring the past to life (Dillon, 2000). Students will gain a better appreciation for their community and its inhabitants and how they go about being productive citizens, "once they realize how people confronted difficulties of earlier time periods" (Van Oteghen, 1996, p.45). Donaldson (1978) argued that children learn content most productively in authentic situations that involve people. Levstik and Barton (1997) asserted:

> The absence of people in the study of history (that) may account for the lack of enthusiasm which has been attributed to the subject. By focusing on people, teachers can both build on what students know best and give them a better sense of what historians actually do. (p. 12)

If students are nervous when interviewing strangers, they can interview people with whom they are more familiar so that they can conduct the project with greater ease and confidence. Parents, friends, parents, grandparents, and neighbors are excellent subjects for interviews (Dillon, 2000; Levstik & Barton, 2005). Many times, the students will find that the individuals they interview are just grateful to be able to share their expertise with others and are extremely willing to share their time.

When conducting an oral history project, a topic of study should be decided upon and research should be conducted prior to any interviews, and some sample questions should be prepared as a focus topic is essential for success. Students should utilize textbooks, letters, diaries, ledgers, newspaper articles, and courthouse and church records to broaden their knowledge of the subject. The questions should be composed after sufficient research has been done so that the interviewer has a better understanding of what questions would be most beneficial, in order for time to be used in the most advantageous way. Frequently, follow-up interviews can be hard to schedule. Practice sessions on how to conduct interviews as well as how to use a tape recorder properly should be held so that the students are as prepared as possible for when the interview actually takes place (Hickey, 1991). It is crucial that the students use a tape recorder so that they can fully concentrate upon the interview rather than having to worry about writing down every word and taking the chance of missing important information or making the subject feel uncomfortable. The tape recorder needs to be tested prior to the interview, and additional equipment should be brought along as backup. Transcriptions of the interview should be written as soon after the interview as possible in order to assure that any additional anecdotal information is recalled and included. These sorts of interviews help to make history more relevant for the students, as they begin to discover from firsthand information that evidence does exist to support what was read in the textbooks and shared in classroom discussions (Van Oteghen, 1996).

The New York University Program in Public History uses its neighborhoods and inhabitants to investigate local history (Bernstein & Mattingly, 1998). They find that when conducting oral histories, "the interviews chronicle facts and experience unavailable in archival repositories" and that the students are able to "match both oral testimony and archival material to produce questions about context that neither source alone would have generated" (Bernstein & Mattingly, 1998, p. 5). Through their research, they find that, for oral histories to be more valuable, they cannot be treated as a one-shot affair, as there is a need for the subjects to be re-interviewed at many points throughout the research process. They note that, through the use of oral histories, the students begin "to think of the 'public' not simply as a target or recipient but as a genuine participant in the work of historical analysis"; the students begin to gain a sense that "the public's experience is where history happens" (Bernstein & Mattingly, 1998, p. 20).

If having students conduct interviews is not feasible, oral histories may often be found in the local history sections in many public libraries, as many have been collected throughout the years and are stored there for save keeping. Frequently, large quantities of audio tapes are stored away in collections at local libraries having never been touched, because they are left there waiting for someone to transcribe them (Allery, 2000).

One of the more interesting and beneficial projects is one in which Sears and Bidlake (1991) wanted to expose their students to the history of their community through the voices of the elderly living within their area. They decided to invite some of the community's retired citizens to their school for tea with their students and were pleasantly surprised when they had 40 guests arrive eager to share their experiences with the children. The project exceeded their expectations, which was exemplified by one student's comment, "I was worried that my person wouldn't say anything, but the only problem I had was getting her stopped" (Sears & Bidlake, 1991, p. 134). Not only did all of the participants enjoy their afternoon tea, but this process also provided an opportunity to gather an enormous amount of information about the economic history, the changing role of women, and social changes of their community, as well as some wonderful anecdotal stories about past community leaders. The "senior citizen tea" gathering also had the positive effect of erasing some of the negative stereotypes students held about senior citizens.

Conducting oral histories allows students a chance to experience historical events vicariously by talking about the past with those who lived through it and who have direct links to the subject matter at hand. By conducting these histories, the remoteness of the past can become more real to the students, which will help them to more clearly understand historical concepts. Additionally, oral histories allow students to encounter several different perspectives on the same topic which will allow them to use their critical-thinking skills to try and decipher them to find the ones that are most closely aligned to how the past in their community may have occurred (Hickey, 1991).

WALKING TOURS OR BUS TOURS

Great amounts of information can be gathered through walking or bus tours (Allery, 2000; Hickey, 1999; Morris, 2006); while at the same time, fantastic images can be captured by students using both still and video cameras (Cooper, 1999; Dudzik, 1999). If proper planning and coordination are done, including the teacher providing transportation and chaperones, some historical organizations will assist teachers in setting up bus tours along with a guide (Allery, 2000). Typically, there is no cost for the tour guide, but any stops along the way may necessitate the coverage of entrance fees. Black and Blake (2001) explain why these organizations and agencies should be utilized for their expertise and extensive knowledge:

> When agencies undertake work with federal funding or permits, such as building a road or bridge or even a large commercial structure, they are required to conduct archaeological investigations of the affected areas. The same is true for state land. Partly for that reason, state historical agencies and organizations conduct much research on local history and archaeology. (p. 247)

When going on a walking tour of the community with students, it is best to have each student create maps of the immediate area around their school which can then be attached on a bulletin board with the school as the center, so students can have a better spatial understanding of their community prior to the actual trip through it (Hickey, 1999). By conducting a walking tour, students can, in addition to learning about the community's history, develop citizenship skills and gain a better understanding of daily experiences of its inhabitants (Morris, 2006). If physically taking students on a tour of the town is not possible, creating a "virtual trip" around the town can be arranged through the utilization of various Internet-based resources, or other communities throughout the world can be visited via the Internet (Wilson, 1997). Many historic towns have virtual tours and lesson plans available for use in the K-16 classroom.

BUILDINGS

Stevens (2001) reminds us that "we are what we build. From the original settlements along the eastern seaboard to the latest housing tracts encroaching on farmlands and open spaces, our values are embedded in our structures" (p. 48). Students are able to learn a tremendous amount about a community by examining the structures that exist within it (Ducolon, 1999). Through careful analysis of the oldest buildings within the community, students can often reveal areas from which the earliest settlers immigrated due to the style and materials used in their building processes, because the earliest settlers "tended to re-create, as faithfully as circumstances permitted, the style of buildings in their former communities rather than invent new styles" (Stevens, 2001, p. 48). In addition, assumptions can be made about what values were important to people at different periods in time due to the positioning of the building, location, and even from symbols and icons visible on the façade (Morris, 2004).

One excellent example of the way in which students can learn about a society is by looking at the vernacular of the housing that exists within a community, such as through an examination of the Northern New England telescope house and barn—a structure unlike any other found in the United States. Students can look at the vernacular of the housing that exists within these communities and hypothesize reasons for why they were originally constructed in such a manner.

Unique vernacular of the building styles are found in almost every location throughout the country (Stevens, 2001) and tell today's generation a lot about what was important or necessary to inhabitants in their community at early moments in time (Morris, 2004). Through investigations about the buildings within the community, students can get a better image of a past time and compare and contrast it to life today (Ducolon, 1999).

CEMETERIES AND HEADSTONES

So much can be learned about the history of an area or even a nation through the act of visiting cemeteries (Bowden, 2006-2007; Capelle & Smith, 1998; Laney, 1986; Mitoraj, 2001; Morris, 2006; "Plot a Lesson," 2000; Stevens, 2001; Spinner, 1980). Through the utilization and examination of local cemeteries, students gain a better understanding of the heritage and social structure of their surrounding community (Spinner, 1980).

Stevens (2001) suggests that cemeteries are an excellent place to encourage students to utilize the basic five W's of good journalism: who, what, where, when, and why. Students can begin by asking themselves *who* the person might have been and what cultures or ethnic roots the person may have exhibited. The *what* question can allow students to figure out what the person's life might have been like, what occupation he or she might have held, or what the family's status might have been, especially since many of the oldest tombstones give more information about the deceased family members than the deceased themselves. Contemplating the *where* question gets students thinking about where the people might have come from or where they might have been in their lives. The question of *when* might seem like a fairly obvious one; although, many times when natural disasters or illnesses occur, tombstones will reflect what might have happened in the immediate area to cause a large number of deaths at the same point in time, which can allow students to make hypotheses about the cause of death. The last of the five W's is the question of *why*, which can sometimes be the most difficult to ascertain from a tombstone.

The students should be encouraged to look at one specific tombstone and try to deduct as much information as possible as to who the person was and how his or her life was lived. Many times, the other tombstones in the surrounding areas of the cemetery will divulge as much information about the individual's life as his or her own tombstone can offer.

Fourth graders, at Luther Lee Emerson School in Demarest, NJ, conducted a yearlong project in which they collected money through different fund raising activities in order to preserve deteriorating gravestones within their local cemetery ("Plot a Lesson," 2000). Many of the headstones date back to the early 1700s when Dutch settlers located themselves in Demarest. The students learned quite a bit about the history of their community, while they made positive contributions to the restoration of historical monuments within their town.

Mitoraj (2001) contends that students could learn a tremendous amount by looking at the location of headstones in proximity to others as well as examining the epitaphs inscribed upon them and symbols or iconography located above or encircling the epitaph, which represents concepts like redemption, salvation, and resurrection. She also uses Colonial literature to exemplify the use of prose during this time period. After the students have spent several weeks reading and examining meanings of Puritan poetry, sermons, and captivity narratives, they once again look at gravestones and better understand the epitaphs, emblems, and icons found upon them. The students find that the headstones can easily be grouped into time periods, as the markings and language upon them change with the evolving morals and beliefs of the time period. She knows that this is time well spent, because "the understandings they gain, the assumptions they draw, and the processes they are involved in will become the foundation for the rest of their study of the way America came to be" (Mitoraj, 2001, p. 86).

A valuable exercise to have students perform when visiting cemeteries is to have them record the age at death of those who are buried there (Spinner, 1980). Once the students return to the classroom, they can create a histogram indicating ranges of ages at death at different intervals of time. Using this information, they can make predictions about life expectancies at different periods in time and can analyze the causes for fluctuations in the life expectancies (i.e., medical advancements, war, illnesses, etc.). Students' hypotheses can serve as an overall representation of what it may have been like in their community during a previous era (Laney, 1986). One other exercise that can be completed, once back in the classroom, is to have the students create epitaphs for their lives thus far or for 50 to 60 years down the line when they have reached the average life expectancy (Laney, 1986; Spinner, 1980).

BUSINESS PARTNERSHIPS, LOCAL HISTORICAL ASSOCIATIONS, AND MUSEUMS

Many times, businesses in the community are willing and able to help local schools in their attempts to create local histories. One of the best ways to get in contact with businesses in your community that would be willing to create partnerships with local schools is to contact the local Chamber of Commerce, as they often have lists of businesses and organizations that have indicated that they would be willing to work with local schools in these sorts of projects.

One of the best resources within a community is the local historical society, especially since the volunteers there will typically come out to schools and give in-school talks and even set up displays (M. A. Anderson, 2003; Hammonds, 1994). In one example, volunteers even came out to a school to recreate the classroom of the past, complete with one-legged stools and dunce caps (Hammonds, 1994).

City, local, and children's museums can often be the best resource when conducting community histories (C. Carson, 1992; Hammonds, 1994; Kletchka, 2004). These museums not only provide the classroom teacher opportunities for external resources when creating community histories; they can provide chances for the students to continue learning about their community through summer workshops and after school programs. Often, carefully designed lesson plans that accompany resources available through the museum are available for classroom teachers at no cost.

ARTIFACTS

An artifact is defined as any object produced or shaped by human craft, especially a tool, weapon, or ornament of archaeological or historical interest; these items give students "a glimpse into the lives of those who created them and an opportunity to consider the technology, tools, and materials available through time" (Library of Congress, 2003, para. 2). The utilization of artifacts in the teaching of history content, especially during community history research, helps teachers motivate and challenge students, and if used properly, "artifact explorations will foster student inquiry and various modes of creative and critical thinking" (Field, Labbo, Wilhelm, & Garrett, 1996, p. 141). Allowing students an opportunity to investigate artifacts from a particular time or location, especially one familiar to the students, helps them to better understand their own relationship to the past (Rule & Sunal, 1997). Field, Labbo, Wilhelm, and Garrett (1996) noted that "When educators engage children in social studies inquiry that focuses children's attention on artifacts that are representative of cultures, historical eras, and geographic location, history becomes meaningful because children have opportunities to construct understanding and build knowledge" (p. 143).

PHOTOGRAPHS

Using photographs in the classroom to learn more about local history is one of the more accessible and creative ways in which a classroom teacher can expose his or her students to their community's past (Barton, 2001; Felton & Allen, 1990; Kirman, 1995; Miculka, 1997). Barton (2001) contends that when examining historical photographs, students will need the most help with drawing together all of their observations in order to arrive at a conclusion about the lives of the people at a particular point in time. He suggests that teachers use probing questions and graphic organizers along with sets of historical images, as these can help the students to develop important skills of authentic historical inquiry. It is important to note that none of this can be done until the process has been properly modeled by the teacher. Barton also finds that for this exercise to be most beneficial it cannot be a one-time experience, as the students will need to repeat the process on more than one occasion with pictures from different time periods. He also points out that it is essential for the students to think about and discuss what they think they might see in the photograph prior to receiving it for examination. This helps to "activate their prior learning as well as compare that knowledge more systematically to the new information from the photographs"(Barton, 2001, p. 280). Once the students have carefully looked at the photo, they should begin to make inferences about what they think is going on and identify the clues found in the photo that led them to that belief. This will lead to an even higher level of analysis, as the students should then draw more general conclusions as to more generalized patterns of life during the time period. Students should have the opportunity to view many different photographs from the same time period and to hear opinions of fellow classmates so that they can determine whether or not their conclusions are valid and believable. Lastly, students should be able to draw from all of their knowledge and findings to create a display or presentation about the time period and geographic area of which they studied. Barton (2001) feels that this is "historical inquiry at its most authentic, because students are making observations from primary sources, drawing conclusions, comparing findings with others, investigating new sources to answer emerging questions, and reporting their findings" (p. 281).

Miculka (1997) suggests that using photographs to look at the past sharpens investigative skills through discovery and analysis of details within the image that no other artifact type can provide. She has also found that she is able to involve the entire class in a more natural conversation about a photograph shortly after it is displayed by showing the image and allowing the class to dictate the flow of the discussion. Miculka finds it helpful to invite a local photographer who deals with restoration and preservation of old photos to visit the classroom and speak to the students about film and preservation processes used to protect older photographs. This may also initiate conversations about the decisions that the photographer must make when capturing a scene and why specific angles and settings are chosen.

Miculka also teaches her students techniques for viewing photographs so that they will gain as much information from each of the images as possible. Her favorite approach is the "clock routine" in which the students are expected to look at each photograph beginning at the twelve o'clock position and continuing around the image in a clockwise pattern. The students are instructed to record any details observed in each of the 10- to 15-minute sections of the image in a sequential manner, which allows them to observe more details as they are only focusing on a small section at a time. Miculka (1997) finds that the use of historical photographs could be a tool that may "spark interest, place the reader in the appropriate place and time, and provide a multitude of possibilities to acquire, analyze, and interpret data. Students learn to organize and record their analysis of a photograph in a systematic way" (p. 10).

One method that Kirman (1995) finds beneficial is to re-photograph scenes in pictures or postcards from earlier times. He feels that several objectives can be explored such as perceiving the amount of change that has taken place over time, examining the impact of technology upon the landscape, and determining the environmental impact that has taken place. Kirman suggests that some of the places in which the original photographs can be found are at government archives, museums, historical societies, and in collections of local, unofficial historians, in old newspapers and magazines, and from family albums. He notes that many local libraries and places of historical interest sell sets of old photographs. When it is impossible to photograph exact locations due to the growth vegetation or buildings or restrictions to the public, you can be creative in finding new angles to photograph the same general area. Kirman (1995) suggests that one could also use similar items such as transportation or schoolhouses throughout time that can exemplify the rate of change that has occurred.

Mouton and Tevis (1991) find that they are able to locate "trays and trays" of old negatives in the photo archives of a local historical museum (p. 13). They try to limit their selection to around 25 of the best representations of life within their town at different times in history. Once images they want to reproduce are chosen, the process of designing a lesson to accompany them begins. They decided that students would be organized into groups of four to six and would begin by examining a single photograph while answering several probing questions. The students then discuss their thoughts and exchange their photographs with a partner group. Both groups examine their new photograph, answer the questions, and discuss their thoughts. Once both groups have sufficient time to look at the two photographs, they come together to create one larger group and discuss the photographs and compare the two as to the dates of each and as to what could be seen in the two photos. Once an ample amount of time is spent conversing about the two images, the students are then able to reveal the true description of the photographs through a narrative previously prepared by the teacher. Through this process, Moulton and Tevis (1991) find that the students are able to recognize details that were unnoticed by the adults who had viewed the photographs. The most striking difference that immediately stood out to the students, as being different from the present day, is the dress of the earlier time periods, especially the buttoned shoes, long dresses, and bib overalls. Given the opportunity to examine the photos, the students are able to delve more deeply into them and find the smallest of details that are easily passed over by their teacher.

POSTCARDS AND GREETING CARDS

Postcards have been in use across the United States since the late nineteenth century and have continued to be abundantly available since (Bucher & Fravel, 1991). The use of postcards in the creation of local histories can be one of the most creative and informative ways to learn about a community, while being relatively inexpensive. The postcards could be used to observe change over a period of time, to create a visual timeline of a section of the town, to describe economic factors that seem to be indicated in the pictures, to study architecture, clothing, transportation, or other factors of an earlier time period, to develop a "then and now" bulletin board of different time periods, or to write letters from the time period describing what life was like for its inhabitants (Bucher & Fravel, 1991).

Copies of postcards can be obtained from historical societies, libraries, or local residents; originals can be bought at antique or thrift stores and flea markets (Bucher & Fravel, 1991) or on eBay at relatively inexpensive prices. Stamped and dated postcards could also be used to prompt inquiry about social customs and how the customs change over time, technological change, as well as costs of postage during different periods in time (Otten, 1998).

One of the most difficult things when working with postcards is to find an exact date of the picture, as it is possible for a photograph to have been taken many years prior to the mailing postmark. Bucher and Fravel (1991) were able to provide some suggestions when working with postcards without a clear date for the photograph:

- Postcards did not have the term "private mailing card" printed upon them until 1898, which is a term still present on some cards today.
- Up until 1907, the U.S. government only allowed messages to be printed on the picture side of the postcard with only mailing information on the reverse.
- "White-border" cards, or postcards that had a white or cream border surrounding the entire photo, were most common in the period between 1916 and 1930 and were gradually replaced with "linens" or cards that were printed on textured, linenlike paper, which were used until 1945.
- Photochrome cards replaced the linens, although they began to be seen in limited use as early as 1939. These are similar to the cards that are still in use today.

Through the use of postcards, Bucher and Fravel (1991) find that "students develop a strong feeling of ownership with their past and become highly motivated to learn about their local community [as] postcards can really make local history come alive" (p. 20).

Levy (1997) suggests that educators have their students write letters to editors of newspapers across the United States asking their readers to send postcards about their community to the class. This allows the students to learn about other communities and, in turn, to learn more about their own neighborhoods through comparison with other areas throughout the United States. In addition, students can learn locations of different communities through the construction of a "Postcards across America" bulletin board displaying the postcards next to their location on a U.S. map.

RADIO

Recordings of radio programs and radio advertisements from the past can be used to teach about the past as it often reflects the influences, tastes, and even moral character of an earlier time period (Turner & Hickey, 1991). Students can also use the audio recordings as the basis for interviews of adults who remember the days of radio to gain better perspectives on life in the past.

One of the best examples of this is a website entitled, "A gullible nation: A closer look at that night of panic" (Grogan, 2007). This site clearly sets the stage for the infamous broadcast of Orson Welles' version of the *War of the Worlds*. It allows the visitor an opportunity to know what society was like during that time period and to examine reasons for paranoia and believability of the broadcast. It does a beautiful job of allowing the user to really understand the circumstances through the use of audio clips of the entire broadcast, as well as other news broadcasts from the time, that can be used for comparison and setting the scene for the state of the nation at that point in time.

Audio recordings can be found on a number of sites on the Internet, in local libraries, museums, and historical societies, as well as for purchase through many different organizations and businesses. By allowing students an opportunity to listen to recordings of old broadcasts and talk to people who remember utilizing radio for receiving information, students can learn a great deal about life in their community and the process utilized by professional historians (Turner & Hickey, 1991).

COMMUNITY SERVICE PROJECTS

Community service projects (CSP), also known as community service learning (CSL), is a process used in education in which students are involved in service experiences within their communities which often can become an excellent way to get the students involved in their own learning processes (Spivey, 2005). Kinsley (1994) most clearly defines CSL as being a service experience that is "directly related to academic subject matter," one that "involves them in making positive contributions to individuals and community institutions"; a final and vital characteristic is that it "requires students to reflect on what they are doing, on what happens, on what that means, and on its importance" (pp. 40-41).

CSP allow students to learn about the history of an area while actively helping others and making a positive contribution to the community and the lives of others. Along with the idea of the incorporation of CSP into history curriculum, the question often arises as to why the children are involved in this sort of process. Kinsley (1994) has two reasons: One is that they get a better education—they learn better, more broadly, and more deeply than in the classroom alone—the other reason is that it changes them as human beings. Through experience and research on the topic of community service learning, Wade (1997) posits that there are some promising trends for the incorporation of CSP into the K-16 curriculum.

Findings, from research conducted by Kinsley (1994), point to the fact that more than nine out of 10 of the CSP students responded that they enjoyed learning a subject more when CSP was used as the learning vehicle. In contrast, just two out of three in the non-CSP group said they enjoyed learning in the non-CSP environment. The evaluation of this project also found that CSP scores were higher than three other types of service learning when it comes to children's social, psychological, and intellectual development.

Ciaccio (1999) notes that there are many benefits to students conducting service-learning projects. The first of which is the feeling of usefulness that the students acquire from their experiences that gives them a sense of personal growth and enhanced self-esteem by becoming more aware of their positive inner characteristics. Also, social skills and critical thinking skills are improved, due to students' needs to solve real-life problems on their own.

The community can be utilized by the classroom teacher as a laboratory in which students can learn more about their local history, as well as other concepts, because many students become more interested in history when they feel as though there is some relevance of the historical content found in textbooks to the real world. Ciaccio (1999) posits that "Far too many schools employ community service only as a sporadic activity when it should be an ongoing K-12 commitment" (p. 63).

FINAL PRODUCTS

In order for the research of a community's history to be something that students are going to be energetic about and have lasting memories, the presentation or final project must be one that will be appealing to the students. The history literature also provides rich descriptions of community history final products (e.g., Churchwell, Weller, & Sommer, 1997; Gilbert, 2001; Hickey, 1999; Making History," 2000; Mitoraj, 2001; Schlumpf & Zschernitz, 2007).

For example, the students at Altoona Area High School in Altoona, PA, spent an entire year investigating, recording information, and publishing stories about their city's past, in conjunction with Altoona's sesquicentennial (Making History," 2000). Each high school student created a website (http://aahs.aasdcat.com/9a) to teach younger students, in the fourth and fifth grade, more about their local community. These interactive, highly visual, stimulating websites included information about their city with images, photographs, and even drawings created by a local artist. The interactive stories published on the Internet allow each user to insert his or her name, as well as the names of other family members or friends, into historical stories, in order to learn more about events that occurred in the past in a more personalized manner. The teachers involved, in this project, received overwhelmingly positive feedback, which inspired students on both ends of the project to want to learn more about their local history. Through the creation of local history websites, accessibility to information and resources is greatly increased (Schlumpf & Zschernitz, 2007), and at the same time, the importance of learning about and showcasing the history of a community is exemplified.

In another example, Hometown Discovery uses a similar approach to teaching younger students about the world around them (Churchwell, Weller, & Sommer, 1997). High school students in Grahamsville, NY, are given the opportunity to take a course as an elective in which they learn more about their community and learn the computer skills necessary to create interactive, interdisciplinary, multimedia presentations that can be used with fourth graders to teach local history. The teachers involved with this project find ways to use their local history to draw connections to the history of the country. The ninth and tenth graders are grouped into production teams of two or three and work with teachers, as well as many different people, businesses, and organizations within their community, to create a final product that recreates events from their community's past.

In another example, Mitoraj (2001) conducts historical inquiry of local cemeteries. Students, with the help of some audiovisual-television technicians, create exhibits and videos including interviews with the caretaker, discussions with the descendents of the people's headstones they were investigating, and clips from the cemetery itself. These videos are broadcasted on their local cable access television station and are archived in their local library within its community history section. These are all beneficial elements of learning, as Mitoraj (2001) asserts:

Students come away from this unit with a sense of empowerment when their project appears on television or showcased for the entire school. Their research has significance. It matters to other students who will read or view the work as models for future projects; it teaches the community what a valuable historic landmark an old burial ground can be, and it gives students a sense of connection with history. (p. 86)

Hickey (1999) suggests that an excellent way to organize the information gathered in a study of a local community is to create a timeline of the major events that occurred within it that may have shaped the way it is seen today. As they create a timeline, students begin to "notice trends, consider cause and effect, and become aware of the chronological relationships between and among events" (Hickey, 1999, p. 75). Many times, you may be able to discover a timeline that has already been created for your community and will be able to add your findings to it, and in other cases, you may need to start from scratch with your own creation.

Through their work at New York University, Bernstein and Mattingly (1998) have their students keep visual logs throughout the process of investigating a community's history. During the process of gathering information, the students are expected to take photographs and images in which they identify and record brief descriptions of the objects even if clear connections for why they were taken are not entirely evident. This process "continually sensitizes each student to the possibilities of visual matter as primary source material" (Bernstein & Mattingly, 1998, p. 13). From all of the logs that have been compiled, students are asked, at different points in time, to draw five or six images for a "TV spot." Bernstein and Mattingly (1998) feel as though the "subject matter of the spot will be the student's own preliminary research argument, but the pedagogical point will be twofold: (1) how images can be used as primary sources, and (2) how visuals serve to carry complex points economically" (p. 14). As a consequence of their research, they find that the majority of the students learn through this process the essential nature of the written word even when images are available. Many of the students rely on recording a great deal about the images, rather than allowing the image alone to carry their argument that was generated, a phenomenon about which Bernstein and Mattingly (1998) speculate:

Exactly what force does an interpretation of the past have if laden with 1990s cultural constrictions? If we automatically assume a criminal record to be a shaming experience, what has been overlooked? To what extent must these time-bound, subjective valuations be acknowledged in historical analysis? (p. 8)

Town-based writing projects can also be used when creating a community history (Gilbert, 2001; Leal, 2003). Gilbert (2001) has her Advanced Placement seniors profile the community, as well as its townspeople, in essays, which are then published and bound into a collection that became a part of the town's 350th anniversary celebration. The collection became the hit of the town and is circulating among its inhabitants so that they can all read about the historical past of their community. Leal (2003) has second graders construct whole class and individually authored books depicting the past of their local community.

CONCLUSION

As educators, a difficult dilemma, but an essential one, is to make the act of learning about history more enjoyable and motivating for our students (Black & Blake, 2001). History is not a boring subject (Jensen, 2001), which is evidenced by the number of top grossing "historical" movies in Hollywood each year. Enjoyment of history is dependent upon how it is taught not necessarily the content (Black & Blake, 2001). Using community histories may be one of the best methods for involving students in their own learning in a manner that can be found extremely enjoyable and relevant for the students completing them (Dillon, 2000; Swiderek; 1997; Waring, 2003; Woods, 2001). Local history projects can be very appealing to students of all ages, especially when including "humorous, heartwarming, shocking, or surprising scenes," while developing the participants into "more than a stereotyped, textbook image of these people" (Kiley & Seifert, 1998, p. 26). Community histories can be conducted in essentially every corner of the world and in most cases without great monetary expense, as many of the resources are available to the general public through libraries, museums, historical societies, and the Internet.

So many other resources can be beneficial when creating local or community history projects that were not addressed in this paper. Some of the other resources that can be utilized when creating community histories are hospitals, churches, schools, observatories, historic sites, farms, construction sites, factories, television studios, waterfronts, military bases, archeological excavations, post offices, fire stations, newspapers, university libraries, and local government agencies (Jensen, 2001; Sprague, 1993). There are also many genealogy organizations that can be contacted whose specific purpose is to investigate family histories and help others trace their family roots and heritage. Teachers could also utilize the Internet, as many resources are available that could be extremely helpful in the construction of a community history project (Clarke & Lee,

2004; Larson, 2001), as well as to add projects of their own (Anderson, 2003; Cooper, 1999).

If we are able to involve students in their own learning process and send them out into the "field," they will be able to experience the processes that social scientists refer to as fieldwork, which means that they will be able to gather information directly from the source rather than secondhand through texts and other such materials (Woods, 2001). Giving students access to their community's past, teachers are more able to "breathe life into dusty facts and forgotten gossip to reveal fascinating sidelights of your town's character" (Kiley & Seifert, 1998, p. 26). If we, as educators, are able to accomplish this, we may find that our students may begin to really enjoy and appreciate history through a process that allows them to tremendously increase their knowledge base of their local community and, at the same time, realize that "people like us make history" (Dillon, 2000).

CHAPTER 9

CONCLUSION

It is critical that students, in history classrooms, have opportunities to experience that which professional historians do and in authentic ways. We know that professional historians write manuscripts, read and comment on other historians' writing, analyze documents, question sources, and delve into archives to find information to help complete the picture of the topic they are studying (Burenheide, 2007). Unfortunately, this is not happening as frequently as we would hope, and students throughout the country find history to boring and unengaging.

This book makes an effort at overcoming the persistent boredom and lack of historical knowledge present in our students, by focusing on ways in which history instruction can be improved:

- detailed instruction on the process of historical inquiry;
- developing historical thinking skills;
- instruction on accessing and examining various primary and secondary sources;
- varied and multiple opportunities to engage in authentic historical inquiry;
- utilizing methods of interest to digital natives;
- providing scaffolds and various ancillary materials to enhance learning;

- investigate history close to the learner (physical—local history; intellectually—what piques his or her interest); and
- constructive assessments.

Additionally, I would suggest that students must have opportunities to ask questions of personal interest. In the process of answering such questions, they should utilize a variety of sources (i.e., published documents, unpublished documents, oral histories, visual documents, artifacts, etc.) to answer the question posed. Each of the sources must be carefully examined to determine who constructed it and why and the context in which it was created. Knowing the context is vital, as a document taken out of context can, and often will, lead to invalid conclusions. Historians, at all levels, read the sources closely and efforts are taken to "read between the lines." Once a picture begins to form, students need to consider alternative perspectives, as finding just the polar extremes or two perspectives is not sufficient. Futhermore, sources that corroborate thoughts need to be found. Finally, multiple and sustained opportunities should be present where students have a chance to construct historical narratives utilizing the spectrum of sources, while noting where gaps in the sources or the author's knowledge exist. If history educators make a concerted effort to combat the persistent distaste and boredom associated with history education with more authentic and engaging methods, we may find a more engaged and interested citizenry who find history to be interesting and one worthy of their time within and outside the classroom.

REFERENCES

Allen, B. P. (1997). *Personality theories, development, growth, and diversity.* New York, NY: Allyn & Bacon.

Allen, J. (1994). If this is history, why isn't it boring? In S. Steffey & W. J. Hood (Eds.), *If this is social studies, why isn't it boring?* (pp. 1-12). York, MA: Stenhouse.

Allery, L. (2000). Popularizing local history services: New century, new ideas. *Australasian Public Libraries and Information Services, 13*(3), 119.

American Psychological Association. (1997). *Learner centered psychological principles: A framework for school reform and redesign.* Washington, DC: Learner Centered Principles Work Group of the American Psychological Association's Board of Educational Affairs. Retrieved from http://www.apa.org/ed/ lcp.html

Anderson, M. A. (2003). Making local history live: A collaborative partnership with a technology base. *Multimedia Schools, 10*(5), 22-23.

Anderson, R. C. (1984). The notion of schemata and the educational enterprise: General discussion of the conference. In R. C. Anderson, R. J. Spiro, & W. E. Montague (Eds.), *Schooling and the acquisition of knowledge.* Hillsdale, NJ: Erlbaum.

Aungst, G., & Zucker, L. (2007). *All about explorers.* Retrieved from http://allaboutexplorers.com/index.html

Avery, B., Avery C., & Williams, C. (1994). You are there: Cooperative teaching makes history come alive. *Social Education, 58*(5), 271-272.

Avery, P. G. (2000). Authentic student performance, assessment tasks, and instruction. *Research and Practice, 8*(1). Retrieved from http://education.umn.edu/CAREI/Reports/Rpractice/ Fall2000/avery.htm

Ayers, E. L. (1999). *The pasts and futures of digital history.* Retrieved from http://www.vcdh. virginia.edu/PastsFutures.html

Bain, R. B. (2006). Rounding up unusual suspects: Facing the authority hidden in the history classroom. *Teachers College Record, 108*(10), 2080-2114.

Bandura, A. (1989). Human agency in social cognitive theory. *American Psychologist, 44*(9), 1175-1184.

Bandura, A. (1999, November). *Laudatio on occasion of the Margaret M. Baltes Legacy Symposium.* Paper presented at the annual scientific meeting of the Gerontological Society of America, San Francisco, CA.

Bandura, A. (2001). Social cognitive theory: An agentic perspective. *Annual Review of Psychology, 52*, 1-26.

Bandura, A. (2002). Social cognitive theory in cultural context. *Applied Psychology: An International Review, 51*(2), 269-290.

Barton, K. (1996). Narrative simplifications in elementary students' historical thinking. In J. Brophy (Ed.), *Advances in research on teaching: Vol. 6. Teaching and learning history* (pp. 51-83). Greenwich, CT: JAI Press.

Barton, K. (1997). History-it can be elementary: An overview of elementary students' understanding of history. *Social Education, 61*(1), 13-16.

Barton, K. (2001). A picture's worth: Analyzing historical photographs in the elementary grades. *Social Education, 65*(5), 278-283.

Barton, K., & Levstik, L. (1996). They still use of their past: Historical salience in elementary children's chronological thinking. *American Educational Research Journal, 28*, 531-576.

Barton, K. C., & Levstik, L. S. (2004). *Teaching history for the common good.* Mahwah, NJ: Erlbaum.

Bell, J. C. (1917). The historic sense. *Journal of Educational Psychology, 8*(5), 317-318.

Bell, J. C., & McCollum, D. F. (1917). A study of the attainments of pupils in United States history, *Journal of Educational Psychology, 8*, 257–274.

Berson, M. J., Berson, I. R., & Iannone, J. L. (2000/2001). Promoting civic action through online resources: An emphasis on global child advocacy. *International Journal of Social Education, 15*(2), 31-45.

Berkin, C. (2008, December). *A brilliant solution: Inventing the American Constitution.* Paper presented at a Teaching American History Symposium, Orlando, FL.

Bernstein, R., & Mattingly, P. H. (1998). The pedagogy of public history. *Journal of American Ethnic History, 18*(1), 77.

Black, M. S., & Blake, M. E. (2001). Knitting local history together: Collaborating to construct curriculum. *The Social Studies, 92*(6), 243-247.

Bohan, C. H., & Davis, O. L. (1998). Historical constructions: How social studies student teachers' historical thinking is reflected in their writing of history. *Theory and Research in Social Education, 26*(2), 173-197.

Bolick, C. M., & Waring, S. M. (2004). Virtual history: Transposing students to another time and place. *Meridian: A Middle School Technologies Journal, 7*(1), 1-5.

Booth, M. (1980). A modern world history course and the thinking of adolescent pupils. *Educational Review, 32*, 245-257.

Bowden, S. H. (2006-2007). Here lies ... cemeteries as historical and artistic lessons for primary-age children: A teacher's K-W-L plan. *Childhood Education, 83*(2), 87-91.

Bradley Commission on History in Schools. (1995). *Building a history curriculum: Guidelines for teaching history in schools*. Westlake, OH: National Council for History Education.

Bransford, J. (2000). *How people learn: Brain, mind, experience, and school*. Washington, DC: National Academy Press.

Brophy, J., & VanSledright, B. (1997). *Teaching and learning history in elementary schools*. New York, NY: Teachers College Press.

Bucher, K. T., & Fravel, M., Jr. (1991). Local history comes alive with postcards. *Social Studies and the Young Learner, 3*(3), 18-20.

Burenheide, B. (2007). I can do this: Revelations on teaching with historical thinking. *The History Teacher, 41*(1), 55-61.

Byron. (Photographer). (c.1900). Italian bread peddlers, Mulberry St., New York, [Online Image]. Retrieved from http://memory.loc.gov/learn/features/port/html/disklp5.html

Caine, R., & Caine, G. (1997). *Education on the Edge of Possibility*. Alexandria, VA: Association for Supervision and Curriculum Development.

Calder, L. (2006). Uncoverage: Toward a signature pedagogy for the history survey. *The Journal of American History, 92*(4), 1358-1370.

Campbell, L. H. (2005). Say it: You can become an oral historian. *Writing, 28*, 8-13.

Capelle, J., & Smith, M. (1998). Using cemetery data to teach population biology and local history. *The American Biology Teacher, 60*(9), 690-693.

Carson, C. (1992). City museums as historians. *Journal of Urban History, 18*(2), 183-191.

Carson, D. C. (2006). *Directory of genealogical and historical societies, libraries, and periodicals in the US and Canada*. Niwot, CO: Iron Gate.

Chapman, A. (2003). Camels, diamonds and counter-factuals: A model for causal reasoning. *Teaching History, 112*, 46-53.

Chi, M. T. H. (1976). Short-term memory limitations in children: Capacity or processing deficits? *Memory and Cognition, 4*, 559-572.

Churchwell, G., Weller, C. J., & Sommer, P. (1997). Hometown discovery: Learning locally, thinking globally. *Technological Horizons in Education Journal, 25*(1), 43-46.

Christen, W. L., & Murphy, T. J. (1991). *Increasing comprehension by activating prior knowledge*. Washington, DC: Office of Educational Research and Improvement.

Ciaccio, J. (1999). The community as lab for service learning. *Education Digest, 65*(5), 63-65.

Clarke, W. G., & Lee, J. K. (2004). The promise of digital history in the teaching of local history. *The Clearing House, 78*(2), 84-87.

Cogan, J., Grossman, D., & Liu, M. (2000). Citizenship: the democratic imagination in a global/local context. *Social Education, 64*(1), 48-52.

Cooper, M. B. (1999). Bringing history home. *Technology & Learning, 20*(2), 68-71.

Cornell University Library. (2006). Five criteria for evaluating web pages. Retrieved from http://www.library.cornell.edu/olinuris/ref/research/webcrit.html

Cuban, L. (1982). Persistent instruction: The high school classroom, 1900-1980. *Phi Delta Kappan, 64*(2), 113-118.

Dawson, K., & Harris, J. (1999). Reaching out: Telecollaboration and social studies. *Social Studies and the Young Learner, 12*(1), 1-4.

den Heyer, K. (2003a). Between every "now" and "then": A role for the study of historical agency in history and citizenship education. *Theory and Research in Social Education, 31*(4), 411-434.

den Heyer, K. (2003b). Historical agency for social change: Something more than 'symbolic' empowerment. In L. Allen, D. Cartner, C. Chargois, R. Gazatamibide-Fernandez, M. Hayes, K. Krasny, & B. Setser (Eds.), *Curriculum and pedagogy for peace and sustainability* (pp. 39-58). Troy, NY: Educator's International Press.

Dewey, J. (1933). *How we think: A restatement of the relation of reflective thinking to the educative process.* New York, NY: D. C. Heath.

Dietz, T., & Burns, T. R. (1992). Human agency and the evolutionary dynamics of culture. *Acta Sociologica, 35*(3), 187-200.

Dillon, P. (2000). Teaching the past through oral history. *The Journal of American History, 87*(2), 602-605.

Donaldson, M. (1978). *Children's minds.* New York, NY: Norton.

Downey, M., & Levstik, L. (1988). Teaching and learning history: The research base. *Social Education, 52*(5), 336-342.

Drake, F. D., & Brown, S. D. (2003). A systematic approach to improve students' historical thinking. *The History Teacher, 36*(4), 465-489.

Ducolon, C. K. (1999). Learning from the buildings around us. *Social Studies and the Young Learner, 11*(4), 27-31.

Dudzik, J. (1999). A marriage made in heaven. *Instructor, 109*(2), 16.

Dunn, R. E. (2000). Constructing world history in the classroom. In P. N. Stearns, P. Seixas, & S. Wineburg (Eds.), *Knowing, teaching, and learning history: National and international perspectives* (pp. 121-139). New York, NY: University Press.

Emirbayer, M., & Mische, A. (1998). What is agency? *American Journal of Sociology, 103*(4), 962-1023.

Erikson, E. (1968). *Identity youth and crisis.* New York, NY: W.W. Norton.

EyeWitness to History. (2001). Battle at Lexington Green, 1775. Retrieved from http://www.eyewitnesstohistory.com/lexington.htm

Facione, P. A. (2004). *Critical thinking: What it is and why it counts.* Milbrae, CA: California Academic Press. Retrieved from http://www.mdaa.org.au/archive/05/manual/app2.pdf

Felton, R. G., & Allen, R. F. (1990). Using visual materials as historical sources: A model for studying state and local history. *The Social Studies, 81*(2), 84-86.

Fertig, G. (2005). Teaching elementary students how to interpret the past. *The Social Studies, 96*(1), 2-8.

Field, S. L., Labbo, L. D., Wilhelm, R. W., & Garrett, A. W. (1996). To touch, to feel, to see: Artifact inquiry in the social studies classroom. *Social Education, 60*(3), 141-143.

Filby, P. W. (1988). *Directory of American Libraries with genealogy or local history collections.* Wilmington, NC: Scholarly Resources.

Fine, B. (1943, April 4). Ignorance of U.S. history shown by college freshmen. *New York Times,* pp. 1, 32-33.

Fiske, E. B. (1976, May 2). Times test of college freshmen shows knowledge of American history limited. *New York Times,* pp. 1, 65-66.

Fuchs, C. (2003). The Internet as a self-organizing socio-technological system. *Human Strategies in Complexity Research Paper.* Retrieved from http://papers.ssrn.com/sol3/ papers.cfm?abstract_id=458680

Fuchs, J. (2006). History detectives. *Teaching PreK-8, 37*(2), 56-57.

Gallavan, N. P., & Kottler, E. (2007). Eight types of graphic organizers for empowering social studies students and teachers. *The Social Studies, 98*(3), 117-123.

Garbarino, J. (1985). *Adolescent development, An ecological perspective.* Columbus, OH: Charles Merrill.

Gilbert, B. (2001). Designing a town-based writing project. *English Journal, 90*(5), 88-92.

Gillette, A. (2006). Why did they fight the great war? A multi-level class analysis of the causes of the First World War. *The History Teacher, 40*(1), 45-58.

Glaser, R., & Resnick, L. (1991). *National Research Center on Student Learning.* Washington, DC: Office of Educational Research and Improvement.

Goldenberg, L. B., & Tally, B. (2005). Fostering historical thinking with digitized primary sources. *Journal of Research on Technology in Education, 38*(1), 1-21.

Grogan, R. (2007). *A gullible nation: A closer look at that night of panic.* Retrieved from http://xroads.virginia.edu/%7E1930s/RADIO/WOTW/frames.html

Gulikers, J. T. M., Bastiaens, T. J., & Kirschner, P. A. (2004). A five-dimensional framework for authentic assessment. *Education Technology Research and Development, 52*(3), 67-86.

Hall, G. S. (Ed.). (1885). Introduction. In G. S. Hall , *Methods of teaching history* (2nd ed.). Boston, MA: Ginn, Heath, & Company.

Halpern, D. F. (2007). The nature and nurture of critical thinking. In R. J. Sternberg, H. L. Roediger, III, & D. F. Halpern (Eds.), *Critical thinking in psychology* (pp. 1-14). Cambridge, NY: Cambridge University Press.

Hammonds, K. (1994). Dig into community resources: Teachers map out great connections you can make in your own hometown. *Instructor, 104*(1), 72-74.

Hartzler-Miller, C. (2001). Making sense of "best practice" in teaching history. *Theory and Research in Social Education, 29*(4), 672-695.

Helmreich, J. E. (1989). The curricular validity of local history: Surface events and underlying values. *Social Education, 53*(5), 310-313.

Hickey, M. G. (1991). And then what happened, Grandpa?: Oral history projects in the elementary classroom. *Social Education, 55*(4), 216-217.

Hickey, M. G. (1999). *Bringing history home: Local and family history projects for grades K-6.* Needham Heights, MA: Allyn & Bacon.

Hicks, D., Carroll, J., Doolittle, P., Lee, J., & Oliver, B. (2004). Teaching the mystery of history. *Social Studies and the Young Learner, 16*(3), 14-16.

Hicks, D., Doolittle, P., & Ewing, E. (2004). The SCIM-C Strategy: Expert historians, historical inquiry, and multimedia. *Social Education, 68*(3), 221-225.

Hicks, D., Doolittle, P., & Lee, J. (2004). Social studies teachers' use of classroom-based and web-based historical primary sources. *Theory and Research in Social Education, 32*(2), 213-247.

Hines, B., & Day, J. (2002). *What do you see?* Retrieved from http://memory.loc.gov/ammem/ndlpedu/lessons/97/civilwar/ hinesday.html

Howard, R. W. (1987). *Concepts and schemata: An introduction.* Philadelphia, PA: Cassell.

Immerwhar, D. (2008). The fact/narrative distinction and student examinations in history. *The History Teacher, 41*(2), 199-205.

International Society for Technology in Education. (2004). *National educational technology standards for students.* Retrieved from http://cnets.iste.org

Jensen, M. (2001). Bring the past to life. *The Writer, 114*(11), 30.

Kiley, M., & Seifert, S. (1998). How to sell local history. *The Writer, 111*(1), 25-26.

Kinsley, C. W. (1994). What is community service learning? Children who can make a life as well as a living. *Vital Speeches, 61*(2), 40-43.

Kirman, J. M. (1995). Teaching about local history using customized photographs. *Social Education, 59*(1), 11-13.

Kleiner, A., & Farris, E. (2002). *Internet access in U.S. public schools and classrooms: 1994-2001.* Retrieved from http://nces.ed.gov/pubsearch/pubsinfo.asp?pubid=2002018

Kletchka, D. C. (2004). Museums, libraries, and public television: Partners in public service. *Art Education, 57*(4), 13-18.

Kliebard, H. M. (2004). *The struggle for the American curriculum, 1893-1958.* New York, NY: Routledge.

Knox, D. (Photographer). (1864). Petersburg, Va. The "Dictator," a closer view, [Online Image]. Retrieved from http://memory.loc.gov/pnp/cwp/4a40000/4a40100/4a40112r.jpg

Laney, J. D. (1986). Learning history from a cemetery: Directed discovery for the intermediate grades. *Southern Social Studies Quarterly, 12*(2), 14-26.

Larson, M. A. (2001). Potential, potential, potential: The marriage of oral history and the World Wide Web. *The Journal of American History, 88*(2), 596-603.

Lave, J., & Wenger, E. (1991). *Situated learning: Legitimate peripheral participation.* New York, NY: Cambridge University Press.

Leal, D. J. (2003). Digging up the past, building the future: Using book authoring to discover and showcase a community's history. *The Reading Teacher, 57*(1), 56-60.

Lebow, R. N. (2007). Counterfactual thought experiments: A necessary teaching tool. *The History Teacher, 40*(2), 153-176.

Lee, J. K. (2002). Digital history in the history/social studies classroom. *The History Teacher, 35*(4), 503-517.

Lee, J. K., Doolittle, P. E., & Hicks, D. (2006). Social studies and history teachers' uses of non-digital and digital historical resources. *Social Studies Research and Practice, 1*(3), 291-311. Retrieved from http://www.socstrp.org/issues/PDF/1.3.2.pdf

Lee, P. (1998). Making sense of historical accounts. *Canadian Social Studies, 32*(2), 52-54.

Leming, J., Ellington, L., & Schug, M. (2006). The state of social studies: A national random survey of elementary and middle school social studies teachers. *Social Education, 70*(5), 322-327.

Levstik, L. (1997). Any history in someone's history: Listening to multiple voices from the past. *Social Education, 61*(1), 48-51.

Levstik, L. S., & Barton, K. C. (1997). *Doing history: Investigating with children in elementary and middle schools.* Mahwah, NJ: Erlbaum.

Levstik, L. S., & Barton, K. C. (2005). *Doing history: Investigating with children in elementary and middle schools* (3rd ed.). Mahwah, NJ: Erlbaum.

Levy, T. (1997). Wish you were here! Postcards across America. *Social Education, 61,* 290-292.

Library of Congress. (2002). *Mindwalk activity.* Retrieved from http://memory.loc.gov/ammem/ndlpedu/lessons/psources/mindwalk.html

Library of Congress. (2003). *What are primary sources?* Retrieved from http://memory.loc.gov/ammem/ndlpedu/start/prim_sources.html

Lockwood, A. L. (1996). Controversial issues: The teacher's crucial role. *Social Education, 60* (1), 28-31.

Lortie, D. C. (1975). *Schoolteacher: A sociological study.* Chicago, IL: University of Chicago Press.

Making history come alive. (2000). *Reading Today, 18*(1), 16.

Marat, D. (2003). *Assessing self-efficacy and agency of secondary school students in a multi-cultural context: Implications for academic achievement.* Proceedings of the New Zealand and Australian Association for Research in Education Conference, Auckland.

Martin, D., & Wineburg, S. (2008). Seeing thinking on the Web. *The History Teacher, 41*(3), 305-319.

Martorella, P. H. (1998a). *Social studies for elementary school children: Developing young citizens* (2nd ed.). Upper Saddle River, NJ: Prentice-Hall.

Martorella, P. H. (1998b). Technology and the social studies or which way to the sleeping giant? *Theory and Research in Social Education, 25*(4), 511-14.

Mason, C., Berson, M., Diem, R., Hicks, D., Lee, J., & Dralle, T. (2000). Guidelines for using technology to prepare social studies teachers. *Contemporary Issues in Technology and Teacher Education, 1*(1), 107-116. Retrieved from http://www.citejournal.org/vol1/iss1/currentissues/socialstudies/article1.htm

McCullough, D. (2005). U.S. history: Our worst subject? Hearing before the United States Senate subcommittee on education and early childhood development of the committee on health, education, labor, and pensions. Retrieved from http://www.gpo.gov/fdsys/pkg/CHRG-109shrg173/html/CHRG-109shrg173.htm

Miculka, L. (1997). Photographs slide into the classroom. *Social Studies and the Young Learner, 9*(3), 8-10.

Milson, A. J. (2002). The Internet and inquiry learning: Integrating medium and method in a sixth grade social studies classroom. *Theory and Research in Social Education, 30*(3), 330-353.

Mitoraj, S. O. (2001). A tale of two cemeteries: Gravestones as community artifacts. *English Journal, 90*(5), 82-87.

Mochizuki, K. (1993). *Baseball saved us.* New York, NY: Lee & Low.

Morris, R. V. (2004). Examples of public and private architecture illustrating civic virtue: Examining local architecture from 1800 to 1850. *The Social Studies, 95*(3), 107-114.

Morris, R. V. (2006). The land of hope: Third-grade students use a walking tour to explore their community. *The Social Studies, 97*(3), 129-132.

Morris, R. V., Morgan-Fleming, B., & Janisch, C. (2001). The diary of Calvin Fletcher: Using primary sources in the elementary classroom. *The Social Studies, 92*(4), 151-153.

Moulton, L., & Tevis, C. (1991). Making history come alive: Using historical photos in the classroom. *Social Studies and the Young Learner. 3*(4), 13-15.

National Center for History in the Schools. (1996). *National Standards for History.* Los Angeles, CA: National Center for History in the Schools.

National Council for the Social Studies. (1994). *Expectations of excellence: Curriculum standards for social studies.* Washington, DC: Author.

National Council for the Social Studies Task Force on Character Education in the Social Studies. (1997). *Fostering civic virtue: Character education in the social studies.* Washington, DC: Author. Retrieved from http://www.socialstudies.org/positions/character

National Council for the Social Studies. (2008). *A vision of powerful teaching and learning in the social studies: Building social understanding and civic efficacy.* Washington, DC: Author. Retrieved from http://www.socialstudies.org/positions/powerful

National Council for the Social Studies. (2010). *About NCSS.* Washington, DC: Author. Retrieved from http://www.socialstudies.org/about

National Research Council, Donovan, S., & Bransford, J. (2005). *How students learn history, mathematics, and science in the classroom.* Washington, DC: National Academies Press.

Newburger, E. C. (2001). *Home computers and Internet use in the United States: August 2000.* Retrieved from http://www.census.gov/prod/2001pubs/ p23-207.pdf

O'Brien, J. E., & White, S. H. (2006). Recapturing the history standards: Historical inquiry in the middle grades. *Middle School Journal, 37*(4), 11-16.

Okolo, C. M., Ferretti, R. P., & MacArthur, C. A. (2007). Talking about history: Discussions in a middle school inclusive classroom. *Journal of Learning Disabilities, 40*(2), 154-165.

Organization of American Historians. (1995). National History Standards, Part I: Standards in Historical Thinking. *OAH Magazine of History, 9*(3), 7-12.

Otten, E. (1998). Using primary sources in the primary grades. *ERIC Digest,* 1-4.

Paul, R., & Elder, L. (2000). Critical thinking: The path to responsible citizenship. *High School Magazine, 7*(8), 10-15.

Penyak, L. M., & Duray, P. B. (1999). Oral history and problematic questions promote issues centered education. *The Social Studies, 90*(2), 68-71.

Piaget, J. (1952). *The origins of intelligence in children.* New York, NY: International Universities Press.

Plot a lesson in community history. (2000). *Curriculum Review, 40*(1), 11.

Pomper, P. (1996). Historians and individual agency. *History and Theory, 35*(3), 281-308.

Prensky, M. (2001). Digital natives, digital immigrants. *On the Horizon, 9*(5). Retrieved from http://www.marcprensky.com/writing/Prensky%20-%20Digital%20Natives,%20Digital%20Immigrants%20-%20Part1.pdf

Purdue University Library. (2006). *Comprehensive online research education online tutorial*. Retrieved from http://gemini.lib.purdue.edu/core

Quest, R. E. (2006). The infusion of local history into the New York State eleventh-grade United States history curriculum. *Dissertations Abstract International, 67*(03), A. (AAT No. 3209986).

Ravitch, D. (1998). Who prepares our history teachers? Who should prepare our history teachers? *The History Teacher, 31*(4), 495-503.

Resnick, L. B. (1987). The 1987 presidential address: Learning in school and out. *Educational Research, 16*(9), 13-20.

Rogoff, B. (1990). *Apprenticeship in thinking: Cognitive development in social context.* New York, NY: Oxford University Press.

Rosenzweig, R., & Thelen, D. P. (1998). *The presence of the past: Popular uses of history in American life*. New York, NY: Columbia University Press.

Rumelhart, D. E. (1980). Schemata: The building blocks of cognition. In R. J. Spiro, B. C. Bruce, & W. F. Brewer (Eds.), *Theoretical issues in reading comprehension*, (pp. 33-58). Hillsdale, NJ: Erlbaum.

Rudd, R. D. (2007). Defining critical thinking. *Techniques, 82*(7), 46-49.

Rule, A. C., & Sunal, C. S. (1997). Buttoning up a hands-on history lesson: Using everyday objects to teach about historical change. In M. E. Haas & M. L. Laughlin (Eds.), *Meeting the standards: Social studies readings for the K-6 educators* (pp. 45-47). Washington DC: National Council for the Social Studies.

Salinas, C., Fraquiz, M. E., & Guberman, S. (2006). Introducing historical thinking to second language learners: Exploring what students know and what they want to know. *The Social Studies. 97*(5), 203-207.

Scheuerell, S. (2007). National history day: Developing digital native historians. *History Teacher, 40*(3), 417-425.

Scheurman, G., & Newmann, F. M. (1998). Authentic intellectual work in social studies: Putting performance before pedagogy. *Social Education, 62*(1), 23-25.

Schlumpf, K., & Zschernitz, R. (2007). Weaving the past into the present by digitizing local history. *Computers in Libraries, 27*(3),10-15.

Schuster, L. A. (2008). Working-class students and historical inquiry: Transforming learning in the classroom, *The History Teacher, 41*(2), 163-178.

Scieszka, J. (1995). *The true story of the 3 little pigs*. New York, NY: Dutton Books.

Sears, A., & Bidlake, G. (1991). The senior citizens' tea: A connecting point for oral history in the elementary school. *The Social Studies, 82*(4), 133-135.

Seixas, P. (1998). Student teachers thinking historically. *Theory and Research in Social Education, 26*(3), 310-341.

Sewell, Jr., W. H. (1992). A theory of structure: Duality, agency, and transformation. *American Journal of Sociology, 98*(1). 1-29.

Shanken, E. A. (2000). Tele-agency: Telematics, telerobotics, and the art of meaning. *Art Journal, 59*(2), 65-77.

Slavin, R. E. (1997). *Educational psychology: Theory and practice* (5th ed.). Needham Heights, MA: Allyn & Bacon.

Solomon, W. (1997). Teaching social studies creatively. In M. E. Haas & M. L. Laughlin (Eds.), *Meeting the standards: Social studies readings for the K-6 educators* (pp. 289-291). Washington DC: National Council for the Social Studies.

Spinner, C. M. (1980). The cemetery and the social studies class. *The Social Studies. 71*(4), 175-177.

Spivey, M. (2005). Service learning: Service through oral history projects. *The Clearing House, 79*(2), 69-70.

Sprague, S. S. (1993). The many faces of local history. *The Historian, 55*(4), 814-820.

Sternberg, R. J., & Horvath, J. A. (1995). A prototype view of expert teaching. *Educational Researcher, 24*(6), 9-17.

Stevens, R. L. (2001). *Homespun: Teaching local history in grades 6-12*. Portsmouth, NH: Heinemann.

Swiderek, B. (1997). Researching local history. *Journal of Adolescent & Adult Literacy, 41*(1), 74-76.

Tally, B., & Goldenberg, L. (2005). Fostering historical thinking with digitized primary sources. *Journal of Research on Technology in Education, 38*(1), 1-21.

Thornton, S. J., & Vukelich, R. (1988). Effects of children's understanding of time concepts on historical understanding. *Theory and Research in Social Education, 16*(1), 69-82.

Torrez, C. F., & Waring, S. M. (2009). Elementary school students, artifacts and primary sources: Learning to engage in historical inquiry. *Social Studies Research and Practice, 4*(2), 79-86.

Turner, T. N., & Hickey, M. G. (1991). Using radio tapes to teach about the past. *Social Studies and the Young Learner, 3*(4), 6-8.

United States Bureau of Education. (1893). *Report of the committee on secondary school studies*. Washington, DC: Government Printing Office.

VanFossen, P. J. (2005). "Reading and math take so much of the time ...": An overview of social studies instruction in elementary classrooms in Indiana. *Theory and Research in Social Education, 33*(3), 376-403.

Van Oteghen, S. L. (1996). Using oral history as a motivating tool in teaching. *The Journal of Physical Education, Recreation, and Dance. 67*(6), 45-48.

VanSledright, B.A. (1998). On the importance of historical positionality to thinking about and teaching history. *International Journal of Social Education, 12*(2), 1-18.

VanSledright, B. (2002). Fifth graders investigating history in the classroom: Results from a researcher-practitioner design experiment. *The Elementary School Journal, 103*(2), 131-160.

VanSledright, B. A. (2004). What does it mean to think historically ... and how do you teach it? *Social Education, 68*(3), 230-233.

Villano, T. (2005). Should social studies textbooks become history? A look at alternative methods to activate schema in the intermediate classroom. *The Reading Teacher, 59*(2), 122-30.

Vogler, K. E., & Virtue, D. (2007). "Just the facts, ma'am": Teaching social studies in the era of standards and high-stakes testing. *Social Studies, 98*(2), 54-58.

Vygotsky, L. (1978). *Mind in society: The development of higher psychological process*. Cambridge, MA: Harvard University Press.

Wade, R. C. (1997). Community service learning and the social studies curriculum: Challenges to effective practice. *The Social Studies, 88*(5), 197-202.

Wang, F. (2001). Subscribing to democracy through the Internet. *The Journal of the Association for History and Computing, 2*(3), 1-21.
Waring, S. M. (2003). Fourth-grade students' experiences during the creation of a technology enriched community history project. *Dissertations Abstract International, 64*(05), A. (AAT No. 3091169).
Waring, S. M. (2005). Digital video editing software and timelines. *Methods and Media, 41*(4), 10.
Waring, S. M. (2006). The agentic power of the Internet. *International Journal of Social Education, 20*(2), 59-72.
Waring, S. M. (2007). Informing preservice teachers about multiple representations of historical events through the utilization of digital resources. *Social Studies Research and Practice, 2*(1), 49-57.
Waring, S. M. (2008). Inquiring about one's community: Conducting community histories with K-12 students. *Social Studies Research and Practice, 3*(3), 86-100.
Waring, S. M. (2008). Teaching democracy to "Digital Natives." In P. J. VanFossen & M. J. Berson (Eds.), *The electronic republic? The impact of technology on education for citizenship* (pp. 161-172). West Lafayette, IN: Purdue University Press.
Waring, S. M. (2009). Using online auctions to invigorate social studies curriculum. *The Social Studies, 100*(2), 93-95.
Waring, S. M. (2010). Escaping myopia: Teaching students about historical causality. *The History Teacher, 43*(2), 283-288.
Waring, S. M., & Robinson, K. (2010). Developing historical thinking skills in middle grades students. *Middle School Journal, 42*(1), 22-28.
Waring, S. M., Santana, M., & Robinson, K. (2009). Making revolutionary movies: The creation of digital biographies in the elementary grades. *Social Studies and the Young Learner, 21*(4), 17-19.
Waring, S. M., & Torrez, C. F. (2010). Using digital primary sources to teach historical perspective to preservice teachers. *Contemporary Issues in Technology and Teacher Education–Social Studies, 10*(3), 294-308.
Wellman, H. M., & Gelman, S. A. (1992). Cognitive development: Foundational theories of core domains. *Annual Review of Psychology, 43*, 337-375.
White, S.H., O'Brien, J.E., Hileman, K., Mortenson, D., & Smith, A. (2006). Build it and they will learn: Creating a history lab in an age of standards. *Middle School Journal, 37*(4), 4-10.
Wiggins, G. P., & McTighe, J. (2001). *Understanding by design.* Upper Saddle River, NJ: Merrill/Prentice Hall.
Wilson, E. K. (1997). A trip to historic Philadelphia on the Web. *Social Education, 61*, 170-2.
Wineburg, S. (1992). Probing the depths of students' historical knowledge. *AHA Perspectives, 30*, 19–24.
Wineburg, S. (2001). *Historical thinking and other unnatural acts: Charting the future of teaching the past.* Philadelphia, PA: Temple University Press.
Wineburg, S. (2010, Winter). Thinking like a historian. *Teaching with Primary Sources Quarterly.* Retrieved from http://www.loc.gov/teachers/tps/quarterly/article.html.
Woodcock, J. (2005). Does the linguistic release the conceptual? Helping Year 10 to improve their causal reasoning. *Teaching History, 119*, 5-15.

Woods, A. (2001). Hey, what's that old chimney over there?: A local history project in Ashville, NC. *Active Learner, 6*(1), 5-11.

Yeager, E. A., & Davis, O. L. (1994). *Understanding the knowing of how history: Elementary student teachers' thinking about historical texts.* Paper presented at the annual meeting of the American Educational Research Association, New Orleans, LA.

Zhao, Y., & Hoge, J. D. (2005). What elementary students and teachers say about social studies. *The Social Studies, 96*(5), 216-221.

ABOUT THE AUTHOR

Scott M. Waring is an assistant professor and program coordinator for the Social Science Education Program at the University of Central Florida. He earned his BS and MA degrees in education from the University of South Florida and a PhD from the University of Virginia in social studies education, with a minor in instructional technology. He teaches elementary and secondary courses at the undergraduate and graduate level in social science education methodology, research, and theory. Additionally, he is the director of the Library of Congress' Teaching with Primary Sources program at the University of Central Florida. While at UCF, Scott has won the University Excellence in Faculty Academic Advising Award, the Award for Excellence in Research, the Award for Excellence in Undergraduate Teaching, and the Award for Excellence in Academic Advising. He is the current chair of the Teacher Education and Professional Development Committee of the National Council for the Social Studies (NCSS) and is vice-chair and chair-elect for the Society for Information Technology & Teacher Education—Social Studies Special Interest Group. In addition, Scott serves as an executive board member for the College and University Faculty Assembly (higher education affiliate of NCSS). He has written or cowritten grants totaling more than $3.3 million, including a Teaching with Primary Sources grant from the Library of Congress and three Teaching American History grants. Scott has multiple journal articles and book chapters published focusing on the teaching and learning of history and the utilization of technology in social science teaching.

www.ingramcontent.com/pod-product-compliance
Lightning Source LLC
Chambersburg PA
CBHW070542300426
44113CB00011B/1767